The Louisiana Coast

Number Fifteen:
GULF COAST STUDIES

SPONSORED BY

Texas A&M University–Corpus Christi
John W. Tunnell Jr., General Editor

The Louisiana Coast

GUIDE TO AN AMERICAN WETLAND

Gay M. Gomez

TEXAS A&M UNIVERSITY PRESS   COLLEGE STATION

This paper meets the requirements
of ANSI/NISO Z39.48-1992
(Permanence of Paper).
Binding materials
have been chosen for durability.

Library of Congress
Cataloging-in-Publication Data

Gomez, Gay M. (Gay Maria), 1956–
    The Louisiana coast : guide to an American wetland /
Gay M. Gomez. —1st ed.
        p. cm. — (Gulf Coast studies ; no. 15)
    Includes bibliographical references and index.
    ISBN-13: 978-1-60344-033-2 (flexbound : alk. paper)
    ISBN-10: 1-60344-033-X (flexbound : alk. paper)
    1. Natural history—Louisiana—Gulf Coast—Guidebooks.
2. Wetlands—Louisiana—Gulf Coast—Guidebooks.
3. Landscape—Louisiana—Gulf Coast—Guidebooks.
4. Chenier plains—Louisiana—Gulf Coast—Guidebooks.
5. Gulf Coast (La.)—Guidebooks.   6. Mississippi River Delta (La.)—
Guidebooks.   7. Gulf Coast (La.)—Environmental conditions.
8. Coastal ecology—Louisiana—Gulf Coast. I. Title.
QH105.L8G66   2008
508.763—dc22   2007048036

Unless noted, all photos are by the author.

To my parents,
Russell and Elizabeth Gomez,
for instilling within me
a love and respect for
Louisiana wetlands,
wetland culture,
and wetland people.
&
In memory of my aunt and uncle,
Beverly and Bubber Thomassie,
who shared our joy
in the coast.
&
For Robert and Rebecca Gomez,
the new generation so far away,
in the hope that you will remember
your Louisiana roots.

Contents

Prelude

Coastal Roots

Although I have traveled on six continents, south Louisiana is my favorite place of all. It is my home by birth and for nearly half a century has been my home by choice. Here I have always lived in cities, but like many working people, I live for the weekends and the chance to breathe air that has a tinge of salt. In other words, I live for my time on the coast.

People define Louisiana's "coast" in different ways. Some see only the twisting line of the shore, where the sea meets the land on sandy beaches or dark mudflats. Others view a large, triangular coastal zone that stretches far up the Mississippi River to the point where its first distributary, the Atchafalaya, carries water southward to the Gulf of Mexico. For the purposes of this book, I define the Louisiana coast as the 20- to 50-mile-wide swath of marshes, swamps, tidal mudflats, beaches, barrier islands, and coastal uplands that lie below the coastwide five-foot land elevation

contour south of U.S. Interstate Highway 10 and Interstate Highway 12. This region south of the Pleistocene Prairie Terrace contains some three million acres of coastal wetlands threaded by ridges of slightly higher land and approximates the area within the Louisiana Department of Natural Resources' coastal zone boundary.

This coast, of course, is much more than a place on a map. It is a place of interaction among land, people, and ideas. It is a home to residents who live along its scant "high" lands, natural levees and isolated ridges that rise above the wetland, sometimes to heights of ten or fifteen feet above sea level. It is a haven to urban dwellers and others seeking recreation and a change of pace. It is a livelihood for thousands who harvest the wetland's wildlife and fisheries and who extract, process, and transport its oil and natural gas. It is a laboratory for generations of scholars and scientists seeking to unravel its complexities. It is a challenge for those working to reverse the erosive forces of wind, wave, tide, and human activity. Because of these many uses and perceptions of the coast, it is often a place of contention and competing interests. Yet it is also a place where people find beauty and peace.

I chose to write *The Louisiana Coast: Guide to an American Wetland* to reveal these layers to anyone who is interested in exploring the state's coastal region. Whether the reader is an armchair traveler or an avid student in the field, I hope this work will provide both information and inspiration, for I have an underlying motive. I want readers to see the coast through my eyes, to fathom its beauty and variety and complexity, and to understand the threat this land, people, and culture face from coastal land loss. I want readers to care about Louisiana's coast as much as I do and to speak and teach and vote on its behalf, for this coast is definitely worth saving.

The Louisiana coast is a place where a tremendous store of knowledge resides, and in this vast lowland I have learned many lessons. The lands, waters, and wildlife of this region have taught me humility, respect, appreciation, and wonder. The people of the coast have shared with me their history, culture, and strategies for adapting to the region's challenges, opportunities, and changes. Land and people, however, are not separate entities, and I have also learned that the essence of the coast lies in the distinctive mark that each places upon the other.

These lessons have been lifelong, and I could only have begun the journey with the love and guidance of those who made the coast a part of my formative experience. My first thanks, then, go to my parents, Elizabeth and Russell Gomez, who shaped my idea of the coast as a place of recreation, relaxation, adventure, and learning. My father, in particular, loved fishing as much as anyone can, and, accordingly, our family spent nearly every weekend at "the camp," which was located first at Lake Hermitage near Myrtle Grove in Plaquemines Parish, then along the Gulf at Grand Isle, then farther inland at Lafitte. Of these places Grand Isle was my favorite, and I will always remember swimming, beachcombing, crabbing, shrimping, fishing, boating, boiling seafood, playing cards, and telling stories with beloved family members and friends. I also treasure the lessons my father taught: not only how to bait a hook, cast a line, and entice fish to bite but also how to ask questions and listen to longtime coastal residents and learn from their many years of experience.

My parents sold the Grand Isle camp during my college years in the mid-1970s, and it was a decade before I returned regularly to the island, this time with binoculars around my neck. My companions on these weekly Sunday journeys were Dan Purrington, David Muth, Buford "Mac" Myers, and the late Norton Nelkin, master birders from whom I learned much about bird migration, behavior, and identification, as well as techniques for finding and calling birds. To these mentors and friends I extend my deepest gratitude for adding a new layer to my experience of the coast, along with a way of interacting with the natural world that has made a positive difference in my life.

My focus shifted to the state's western coast in the 1990s, when I embarked on a study of the Chenier Plain of southwestern Louisiana as part of my dissertation research in the Department of Geography at the University of Texas. I thank Drs. Robin Doughty, Karl Butzer, Bill Doolittle, and others in that department for their support and guidance as my "wetland biography" of the chenier region took shape. I am also grateful to Shannon Davies, then with the University of Texas Press, for shepherding me through the publication process that transformed the dissertation into my first book, *A Wetland Biography: Seasons on Louisiana's Chenier Plain.*

That book, and this one as well, would not have been possible with-out my many friends and teachers in the chenier region, from whom I have learned so much. In addition to teaching me about their land, culture, history, and perceptions, they offered me friendship, hospitality, and inclusion in the activities and events of daily life, which is often the best teacher of all. The Booth, Theriot, Nunez, Trahan, and Little families, among others, welcomed me as one of their own, as did the staff of the Rockefeller State Wildlife Refuge in Grand Chenier, which still feels like "home." To them and to all of the wetland dwellers, users, and managers who assisted me then and from whom I continue to learn, I offer my sincere thanks.

While I would have loved to have spent every minute in this coastal region, the necessity of earning a living is an inescapable reality, and in this context I thank my colleagues at McNeese State University in Lake Charles, Louisiana, where I have taught geography for nearly a decade. I appreciate their support and confidence. The idea to write a second book dawned during my time at McNeese, and I am grateful to the university for granting me a sabbatical year in which to complete the manuscript.

I am indebted as well to Shannon Davies and the staff at Texas A&M University Press for their interest in this guide, and to Drs. Paul Coreil and Bob Thomas, who offered inspiring words and helpful suggestions that improved the work. Clifford Duplechin Jr., cartographic manager for Louisiana State University's Department of Geography and Anthropology, skillfully executed the maps for this guide, while Nancy Mayberry, visual information specialist for the U.S. Army Corps of Engineers, New Orleans District, provided photographs and diagrams that filled gaps in my personal collection of coastal images. I appreciate their generosity, including the gift of their time.

In summary, I am grateful to many individuals, and to the coast itself. Beyond the facts, the images, and the experiences, the Louisiana coast is something more to me. It is the part of me where I find peace. Free of human distractions, I can be truly free, truly quiet; here I can simply be. Amid the tapestry of land, water, and wildlife, I am reminded that I am only a small part of creation. Here, on a good day—when I am really quiet and really listening—my spirit merges with something greater than myself, and I am renewed. I hope there will always be a coast, for me and for all of us.

The Louisiana Coast

CHAPTER 1

The Louisiana Coast
Vital, Valuable, and Vulnerable

L OUISIANA'S COAST is a special place. The vast extent and variety of wetlands here are unparalleled anywhere in the temperate regions of North America. Marshes that span up to forty miles from north to south extend along the state's southern perimeter, while the Atchafalaya Basin, the continent's largest river basin swamp, bisects the marsh and has long served as a physical divide between southwest and southeast Louisiana. Stretching across the parishes of Cameron and Vermilion in southwest Louisiana is the Chenier Plain, an unusual geological formation of extensive marshes crossed by tree-covered ridges; it is one of only three major chenier plains in the entire world. In the southeastern part of the state lies the network of bayous, natural levees, cypress swamps, marshes, bays, and barrier islands of the Deltaic Plain, formed where the Mississippi River has deposited sediment in a series of deltas during the past seven thousand years.

A Vital Region

This varied coast is a vital region in several ways. It is a living land that is continually changing as the Mississippi River, the Gulf of Mexico, and human activities shape and reshape it. It is a human landscape as well as a physical place, a multiethnic region alive and evolving as it has been for centuries, as people use and modify the land and its resources. There is a wealth of experiential knowledge here, for generations have searched for and in many cases have found ways to harness the region's abundance, cope with declines, and meet additional challenges imposed by weather, climate, insect pests, and market downturns. The cultural processes of adaptation, impact, and learning are ongoing on the Louisiana coast, for this is no mere museum or tourist attraction. While the region contains a national park and many state and national wildlife refuges, it remains a true "working wetland," a place that has much to teach and

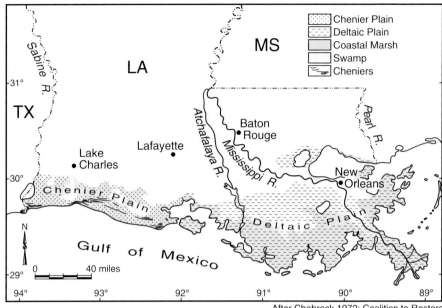

After Chabreck,1972; Coalition to Restore
Coastal Louisiana, 2000

Louisiana Coast

much to give to the entire nation. These gifts include a rich contribution to the nation's energy supply, seafood industry, port and navigation network, and folk culture.

A Valuable Region

"America's Wetland" is a name that the Louisiana coast proudly carries, for this hard-working region makes a significant contribution to the United States and its citizens. The Coalition to Restore Coastal Louisiana's report *No Time to Lose: Facing the Future of Louisiana and the Crisis of Coastal Land Loss* (1999, rev. 2000) and the

Louisiana Department of Natural Resources' publication *America's Energy Corridor* (2006) provide statistics that illustrate these contributions and reveal what is at stake for the state and the nation.

In an age of reliance on hydrocarbon-based energy, Louisiana's wetlands and Gulf waters off the state's coast by the year 2000 furnished an estimated 17 percent of the country's crude oil and 25 percent of its natural gas. In 2006, the Louisiana Department of Natural Resources reported that the production of crude oil and natural gas from the coastal and offshore areas, including wells on the Outer Continental Shelf, ranked Louisiana first and second, respectively, among the fifty states. A vast network of pipelines beneath these lands and waters carries both domestic production and additional, imported oil and gas to the nation's refining and processing facilities. By 2006, the Louisiana coastal area and its associated energy facilities were accommodating the movement of more than 26 percent of the country's crude oil supply, along with more than 26 percent of its natural gas. These percentages will likely increase as offshore oil production expands and additional liquefied natural gas (LNG) receiving terminals begin operations.

In addition to providing energy to the nation, the state's coastal wetlands also support a valuable commercial and recreational fishing industry. While sport fishing is important to the state's economy and culture, the commercial fishing industry is important to the entire nation, for Louisiana's commercial fishermen harvest 25–35 percent of the country's total catch. In 1998, four Louisiana ports—Empire-Venice, Cameron, Intracoastal City, and Morgan City–Berwick—brought in approximately 950 million pounds of seafood; these four consistently rank in the nation's top ten fishing ports by volume of fish and shellfish landed. Along with neighboring ports, their catch includes brown shrimp, white shrimp, blue crabs, oysters, menha-

The number and variety of oil and gas production platforms and drilling rigs off the Louisiana coast bear witness to the state's contribution to the nation's energy supply. While these platforms south of Port Fourchon are visible from shore, many others lie beyond sight in the Gulf of Mexico's deeper waters.

Shrimp boats rigged for trawling in the Gulf of Mexico cluster at docks with ice houses and facilities for off-loading and selling the catch. Vessels like these along the Mermentau River at Grand Chenier sought other ports after Hurricane Rita destroyed the "shrimp house" there.

den, and a variety of edible fish. This catch consistently ranks the state at or near the top of the national harvest of oysters, crabs, and shrimp and first in the harvest of menhaden, a small, inedible fish that processors convert into high protein fish meal and oil. Menhaden has become a major component of feeds for poultry, hogs, mink, cattle, fish farms, and pets and is a valuable export item.

Processed menhaden meal and oil—along with agricultural products, manufactured goods, petroleum products, and a variety of other trade items—pass through south Louisiana's four major shipping facilities: the ports of New Orleans, Greater Baton Rouge, South Louisiana, and Lake Charles. These ports carry nearly 500 million tons of waterborne commerce annually—19 percent of the country's total—including trade passing between the U.S. interior and foreign nations. The four port facilities, as well as major navigation channels such as the Gulf Intracoastal Waterway, are protected from the erosive force of the Gulf's waves by Louisiana's coastal wetlands.

Many south Louisiana residents, including those in New Orleans and other cities near the coast, also rely on these wetlands for protection. Coastal marshes provide a crucial buffer that can reduce a hurricane's wind velocity and its storm surge, the wall of seawater pushed ahead of the hurricane that is often the storm's most destructive force. The presence of a coastal wetland buffer reduces hurricane damage and associated insurance payments and federal assistance costs. Hurricanes Katrina and Rita, which struck the Louisiana coast in 2005, revealed painful lessons about the importance of an intact wetland buffer, as well as the staggering price of coastal wetland loss.

The residents who have for generations weathered hurricanes and reaped the region's bounty are as varied in ethnicity as the coastal region is varied physically. Louisiana's coastal residents include Native Americans, primarily members of the Houma and Chitimacha tribes; Cajuns, descen-

Summer's heat and humidity give rise to spectacular thunderstorms that freshen the wetlands with rainfall and provide energy and moisture for tropical cyclones. Wetlands such as these in Cameron Parish serve as a buffer for inland areas when tropical storms and hurricanes strike the coast.

dants of French-speaking Acadians exiled from Nova Scotia (*Acadie*) by the British in 1755; Isleños, descendants of Spanish-speaking Canary Islanders who arrived in Louisiana in the late 1770s; Croatians (formerly Yugoslavians), who developed the state's oyster industry in the southeastern parishes after their arrival in the early to mid-1800s; African Americans, many of whose ancestors arrived as enslaved peoples before 1865; and a host of others, including Chinese, Filipinos, Germans, Irish, Italians, non-Cajun French, Mexicans and other Latin Americans, Vietnamese, Cambodians, and Anglo-Americans.

This "multicultural gumbo" of people in the coastal region may surprise readers who think of the area as a hearth of Cajun culture, including food, music, cooking techniques, language, and regional accent. Paradoxically, both the varied ethnicity and the strong presence of the Cajun culture are present in and characteristic of the region; they exist simultaneously.

Although some non-Cajun ethnic enclaves were present historically in the more remote areas of the coast, such as the Filipino shrimp-drying platforms of Manila Village in Barataria Bay, today only the Isleño and Vietnamese enclaves cling tenuously to survival. The oldest of these, the Isleño community in southeast Louisiana's St. Bernard Parish, received a severe blow when Hurricane Katrina flooded its lands and homes in 2005, scattering residents and destroying livelihoods. The community is struggling to recover and retain its identity. Several Vietnamese communities, begun by immigrants who came to south Louisiana after the Vietnam War, are located in eastern New Orleans and across the Mississippi River in the metro area's westbank suburbs. The eastern New Orleans enclave was the most severely affected by Hurricane Katrina; it suffered the effects of wind and water, as well as the city's placement of a massive storm debris landfill on its borders.

In other areas, the Cajun settlers not only were numerous but also embraced people of other cultures, intermarrying and absorbing them into the Cajun way of life. This has resulted in a distinctive south Louisiana Cajun culture that extends from the former prairie regions of southwest Louisiana through the coastal areas of the Deltaic Plain and the Chenier Plain. These physical regions have imparted a strong sense of place and identity to their longtime residents; it is an identity rooted in land and resource use, with wildlife harvest, fishing, and petroleum extraction among

An ancient live oak on Cheniere-au-Tigre dwarfs Berton Legé, whose family's roots on the Louisiana coast are as deep as the tree's.

its major components, especially in the coastal areas. Once maligned, the Cajun culture is now a recognized and valued part of the state's and the nation's cultural mosaic.

A Vulnerable Region

The Louisiana coast that supports this culture, however, is a fragile place. Hurricanes threaten it; flood control levees (raised banks) along the Mississippi River starve it of sediment; canals necessary for navigation and oil- and gas-well access provide conduits for saltwater intrusion; subsidence takes its toll. As wetland plants die, land washes away and becomes open water. Oil and gas pipelines, storage tanks, and other facilities nestled within the protective marsh zone become vulnerable as erosion exposes them to the ravages of waves. As wetlands are lost, so too is habitat for a variety of wildlife, from ducks and egrets to alligators, muskrats, and turtles. Lost too are nursery grounds for commercially valuable fish and shellfish, including shrimp, crabs, redfish (red drum), and speckled trout.

Land and culture, of course, are intimately connected, and it is rare that one suffers without the other. For example, as a result of the combination of low dockside prices and the toll of hurricanes on the marsh and the fleet, many families who have earned a livelihood from the seafood industry for generations hang up their nets, sell their boats, close their buying houses and packing companies, and turn to employment in service-sector occupations; some leave the wetland altogether. As wetlands subside and saltwater reaches farther into estuaries, communities face diminished hurricane protection and concerns about salinization of their water supply. Insurance for homes, businesses, and other investments becomes harder and more expensive to obtain as protective wetlands disappear. For some, a move away from the coast is the only viable alternative.

Subsiding wetlands and saltwater intrusion threaten land, resources, and cultural continuity. Fortunately, as an increasing number of government officials, corporate decision makers, environmental activists, and ordinary citizens have become aware of these threats, action has begun to slow the tide of coastal wetland loss. Freshwater- and sediment-diversion projects and saltwater intrusion control (water management) structures have helped lower the coastal land loss rate from an estimated forty square miles per year in the 1980s to approximately twenty-four square miles per year between 1990 and 2000. Restoration programs such as the Coast 2050 Plan and the Louisiana Coastal Area (LCA) Plan have

A subsiding marsh fragments into myriad islands as it sinks slowly beneath the sea. Courtesy of U.S. Army Corps of Engineers, New Orleans District.

evolved into a post-Katrina successor, the Louisiana Coastal Protection and Restoration Authority's Integrated Ecosystem Restoration and Hurricane Protection Master Plan. While state officials seek federal funding to initiate the Master Plan, some of the projects of the Coast 2050 and LCA plans are already operating and are proving their merit in restoring damaged wetlands. The future of the Louisiana coast and its people will depend heavily on the success of these and future restoration efforts.

A Guide to the Coast

The Louisiana coast's variety, vitality, value, and vulnerability are the inspiration for this book, which is part field guide, part nature writing, and part call to action on behalf of the state's vanishing wetlands. *The Louisiana Coast* portrays the region from a geographical perspective; it includes words and images that illustrate components of this special place evident in the landscape, such as flora and fauna and human use of the land

Life on the coast is not without risk, and people who build near the shoreline sometimes lose both homes and property. Courtesy of U.S. Army Corps of Engineers, New Orleans District.

and its resources. The book also illuminates contexts of these components by highlighting the interaction of land, people, and ideas that gives the place its distinctive character.

While this chapter has introduced the Louisiana coast in terms of its variety, vitality, value, and vulnerability, chapter 2 delves into its two broad regions, the Deltaic Plain and the Chenier Plain, in greater detail. Chapters 3 through 5 describe and illustrate coastal plants, animals, and human activities; they focus on major natural and cultural components that one would commonly encounter through observation with the unaided eye. Chapter 6 details an issue critically important to the future of all of these components: coastal land loss and restoration.

No regional study is complete without firsthand experience, and chapter 7 suggests places where readers can explore Louisiana's coastal wetlands and will likely encounter the plants, animals, and human activities described here. The field guide presents some observations on the region's past, present, and future in chapter 8, followed by a list of books and other resources on the Louisiana coast. These works include a selection of detailed field guides suitable for observers with binoculars and a heightened interest in specific aspects of the natural environment, such as birds or wildflowers.

Scientific names of plants and animals may prove useful for identification when a common name is unfamiliar to the reader. Accordingly, scientific names are included in the main photo caption for each species in the vegetation and wildlife chapters; they may also appear in a preceding or subsequent chapter if a species of note is illustrated there but not elsewhere.

Where the Guide Leads

What is the purpose of attaining a better understanding of Louisiana's coast? With knowledge comes power: the power to appreciate and to care, the power to protect and defend, and the power to shape attitudes and

Healthy wetlands are nurturing habitats for a variety of wildlife. A willet—a large, gray, long-billed shorebird—built its nest in this marsh near Johnson Bayou.

practices that will effect a promising future for land, water, and wildlife, as well as for people. Louisiana's coast is in need of such care and protection, not only from Louisianians, but from people around the nation. Every citizen, every voter, and every decision-maker in government, industry, and economic development has a responsibility to care for the health of the land and water, which provide the physical base that supports a people and their culture. The contributions of Louisiana's coastal region to the state and to the nation merit nothing less than our attention and assistance as we work to ensure the survival of this special place.

CHAPTER 2

Deltaic Plain and Chenier Plain Landscapes

L OUISIANA'S COAST is a gift of the Mississippi River. During the past seven thousand years, North America's most extensive river system has carried sediment from approximately two-thirds of the continent and deposited this fluvial treasure in south Louisiana, creating a coastal zone with two distinct regions, the Deltaic Plain and Chenier Plain. Where are these regions located? How are they alike? How do they differ? What reasons account for their similarities and differences? This chapter explores these questions via journeys from three perspectives: a bird's-eye view, a geohistorical look, and a trek at ground level.

An Aerial Journey

An observant airline traveler flying along the coast on a clear day notices aspects of the area's topography that would also catch the eye of a migratory songbird seeking a place to land, rest, and refuel. Both airborne travelers, perhaps because they are ultimately reliant on terra firma, might ask the conscious or instinctive questions "Where is the high land?" and "Where are the trees?" Eyes cast downward, each searches for these two landscape features and finds a distinct difference in their pattern and distribution as the journey progresses.

The first realization is that "high land" in coastal Louisiana is a relative term. There is no visible relief here. There are no discernible hills and valleys, no undulations in the landscape; from the air, everything appears flat. This is due to the fact that "high land" may be no higher than fifteen feet above sea level, in contrast to "low land," which may be five feet or less in elevation. This seemingly small difference, however, makes a world of difference in what vegetation will grow on these lands, for soil type and drainage are intimately tied to the land's elevation above the sea.

On the lower lands, water-tolerant grasses grow, forming marsh habitats.

On the higher, better drained lands, trees such as oaks and hackberries flourish. In the intermediate elevations, baldcypress and water tupelo trees rise from the inundated soil to create swamp forests. Trees, then, offer a cue to the airborne traveler that land of higher elevation lies below. Upland trees signal the presence of relatively high, dry, habitable land. While shining water beneath the feathery needles of cypress trees indicates the presence of swampland, one side of the swamp usually lies adjacent to land of higher elevation. As the aerial journey proceeds from east to west, distinctive patterns of trees and high land emerge as a signature of Louisiana's two coastal regions, the Deltaic Plain and Chenier Plain.

In the southeast and south central parts of the state, from the Pearl River to Vermilion Bay, lies the Deltaic Plain. The high land of this region occurs in narrow strips that hug the

A satellite image of the southeast and south central Louisiana coast reveals the distinctive features of the Deltaic Plain, including the Mississippi River's sediment stream, the chain of barrier islands, and the natural levees that flank the river and major bayous. The large island at left is Marsh Island, an ancient delta remnant, and to its northeast is the Atchafalaya Basin. Courtesy of U.S. Army Corps of Engineers, New Orleans District.

banks of the major rivers and bayous; from the air, these strips of land appear like the downward-pointing fingers of an outstretched, skeletal hand. These strips mark the "natural levees," raised areas of earth that formed when the river or bayou flooded and deposited its largest particles of sediment on the banks nearest the waterway. While most of this high, nutrient-rich land has been cleared for human habitation, agricultural fields, and industrial sites, a few scattered areas of oak-dominated upland forest remain, along with trees associated with parks and residential neighborhoods.

Looking away from the waterways' banks, the airborne traveler surveying this part of the coast finds that the high land first gives way to a watery forest of swamp trees such as baldcypress, then the trees thin and disappear entirely as the land sinks into the grassy wetland of the marsh. Bays mark the mainland's end, but the Deltaic Plain features a string of barrier islands that fringe the coast and protect it from the ravages of storms. If these islands are wide and high enough, they will also support trees, including the signature species of Louisiana's coastal uplands, the live oak.

As the traveler flies westward, a great divide appears. It is the twenty-mile-wide swath of the Atchafalaya Basin, the continent's largest river basin swamp. The basin stretches from north to south along both sides of the Atchafalaya River, the Mississippi's first major distributary. While tributaries to the north pour their water and sediment into the Mississippi, the Atchafalaya pulls muddy water from the great river and carries it toward the Gulf of Mexico 140 miles away. Although the basin's upper reaches are drained and cultivated, and a massive water control structure limits the amount of water flowing from the Mississippi into the Atchafalaya, the basin's central and lower reaches form a vast floodplain dominated by baldcypress and water tupelo trees. Not surprisingly, ornithologists have documented high concentrations of Neotropical migratory birds nesting in this extensive forested haven.

West of the Atchafalaya's mudflat delta, an active delta where land is currently rising from the Gulf, the traveler finds Vermilion Bay. The bay is easy to recognize, for it features the landmark Marsh Island at its center. This large island is aptly named; it is the low-lying remnant of a much older delta and is carpeted with marsh grass. Vermilion Bay and Marsh Island mark the western edge of the Deltaic Plain.

Farther west lies the zone of extensive marshes and ancient beach ridges known as the Chenier Plain. This southwest Louisiana coastal region

Timbalier Island, located south-southeast of Houma, is one of several barrier islands that arc across the entrance to Timbalier Bay and Terrebonne Bay. Timbalier's Gulf side is fringed with a sandy beach that shelters marshland on the island's bay side. Courtesy of U.S. Army Corps of Engineers, New Orleans District.

between Vermilion Bay and Sabine Pass appears much different from the neighboring wetlands. Rivers, bayous, and natural levees are fewer. There are no barrier islands. The coastal region is narrower from north to south, and its shoreline appears smooth rather than ragged. There are four large lakes here; the human traveler can identify them on the map, from east to west, as White Lake, Grand Lake, Calcasieu Lake, and Sa-

bine Lake. Unlike the Deltaic Plain, this wetland has no large swamp forests, only a few isolated stands of baldcypress and tupelo along some of the rivers and bayous.

What is extensive in the Chenier Plain is marshland, which stretches from north to south for twenty to thirty miles. Crossing this vast marsh is the region's most striking topographic feature, the cheniers. From the air, cheniers appear as long, narrow, roughly parallel lines of higher land that cross the marsh from east to west, like threads spread horizontally across a cloth. These upland ridges give the region its name, as well as its distinctive character.

The cheniers stand out to the airborne traveler, for they are clad in trees, including the broad, dark green canopy of the live oak. The oak, in fact, gave its name to these ridges, for the term "chenier" comes from the region's early French-speaking inhabitants, who named the ridges for the trees that were so prominent there. The French word for "oak" is *chêne,* and a *chênière* is a "place of oaks." Geologists who studied the area in the 1930s appropriated the local name for these ancient beach ridges,

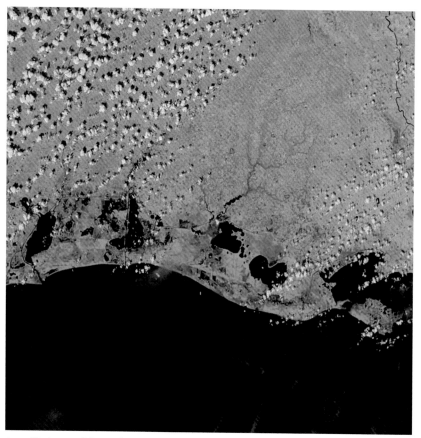

A satellite image of the southwest Louisiana coast depicts the four large lakes of the Chenier Plain. Geologists believe the lakes were once bays that were blocked by sediment from the Mississippi River as the Chenier Plain formed. Courtesy of U.S. Army Corps of Engineers, New Orleans District.

Oak-covered chenier ridges usually run parallel to each other, for they mark the location of former shorelines. Near the banks of rivers or lakes (former bays), however, closely spaced ridges often diverge, creating a fan-shaped appearance. Courtesy of U.S. Army Corps of Engineers, New Orleans District.

and the terms "chenier" and "chenier plain" are now part of the geological vocabulary.

The cheniers of the state's southwest coast and the natural levees and barrier islands of the southeast and south central coast represent for the airborne traveler—bird or human—a safe landing place amid the watery lowlands of coastal Louisiana. Songbirds and other migrants crossing the Gulf in spring or preparing for their southerly journey in fall seek such places to rest, feed, and drink fresh water. It is possible at times, such as during and after a spring storm, to see large numbers of these birds seek-

ing refuge in the coastal woodlands. Without these places, however, a bird may perish; conservationists have noted the importance of such areas in the survival not only of individuals but of species as well.

Humans also need healthy coastal habitats. They provide our dwelling places, our places of business and industry, our places of recreation. We breathe the air and drink water from their rivers, bayous, and aquifers. The Deltaic Plain and Chenier Plain, though different in some landscape features, are similar in providing a mosaic of lowlands and uplands that serve as a physical base for human activity and culture. How did this extensive and varied physical base come to be? To answer this question, we shift from air travel to time travel as we explore the geologic formation of the state's two coastal regions.

Coastal Origins

Any exploration of Louisiana's coastal genesis begins with the Mississippi River. According to Rand McNally's *Atlas of World Geography,* this vast waterway, along with its tributaries, constitutes the world's third largest drainage basin (1,243,000 square miles) and fourth longest river system (3,740 miles). An alluvial river that carries sediment from such a broad region has enormous potential for land building along its lower course.

During the past seven thousand years, the Mississippi has lived up to its potential by forming the land we know today as coastal Louisiana. Along the river's southern reaches, the current slowed in response to flatter terrain, the river meandered, and spring floods occurred as melting snows from higher, distant parts of the basin poured additional water into the river system. These annual floodwaters carried millions of tons of sediment that covered the land with nutrient-rich mud. Larger particles of this sediment settled along the banks of the waterway, raising them higher

and forming natural levees, while smaller particles were carried farther away from the river's channel. When the river retreated from its floodplain, a blanket of soil remained, fertilizing the land and building it upward.

At the river's mouth, a constant and accelerated process of sediment deposition formed mudflats that built not only upward but outward, converting open water to low-lying wetlands. As land continued to rise from the Gulf, saltwater-tolerant vegetation began to colonize the innermost mudflats and hold the soil in place, forming new marshes. As centuries passed, additional layers of sediment added elevation and extended the coast outward in a broad delta.

Because the Mississippi has shifted course at least four times since the end of the last Ice Age, five broad deltas overlap to form the Deltaic Plain. These deltas are the Sale-Cypremort or Maringouin (active ca. 7,300–6,000 B.P.), Teche (6,000–2,500 B.P.), St. Bernard–Barataria (4,600–700 B.P.), Lafourche (3,500–400 B.P.), and Plaquemines-Balize or Modern (1,000 B.P. to present). Notice that the time periods of these deltas overlap, indicating that new deltas were beginning to grow even as the river's main course was slowly abandoning the old delta region. This process is occurring today as well, for the Atchafalaya River has been creating a delta in Atchafalaya Bay since 1973,

The Mississippi River delta builds where sediment spreads outward and vegetation anchors the soil in place. Slightly higher elevations support the growth of trees, while lower-lying land is carpeted in marsh grass. Courtesy of U.S. Army Corps of Engineers, New Orleans District.

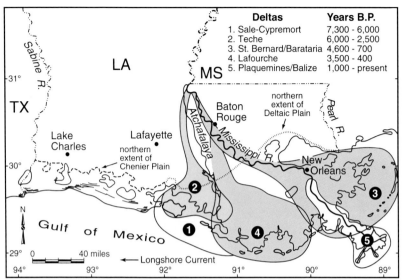

Deltas	Years B.P.
1. Sale-Cypremort	7,300 - 6,000
2. Teche	6,000 - 2,500
3. St. Bernard/Barataria	4,600 - 700
4. Lafourche	3,500 - 400
5. Plaquemines/Balize	1,000 - present

After Saucier, 1994; Frazier, 1967

Shifting Deltas of the Mississippi River

even as the Mississippi's main channel remains constrained in its present course.

Each of the five deltas marks the river's shift to a shorter, steeper route to the Gulf, but the remnants of the river's former main channels remain in the landscape of coastal Louisiana. The small, sluggish stream of Bayou Maringouin, for example, winds through the central coast just east of the Atchafalaya River and marks this ancient course of the Mississippi as it built the Maringouin delta. ("Maringouin" is Louisiana Cajun French for "mosquito.") Other old river channels include Bayou Teche and Bayou Lafourche, which lie west and east of the Atchafalaya Basin, respectively, and Bayou Barataria, which drains

lands south of New Orleans. Each of these bayous flows slowly southward to the Gulf. In fact, the native Choctaw word "bayou" refers to a slowly moving waterway, an accurate description for the streams the Mississippi has abandoned. Along these old river courses lie the Deltaic Plain's fingerlike pattern of natural levees, beyond which are swamp forests, marshes, bays, barrier islands, and the Gulf of Mexico.

Not every particle of mud settled in the river's delta, however. Smaller, lighter particles, especially clays, were carried westward from the Mississippi's mouth, propelled by the longshore current that flows east-to-west along the Gulf's northern shores. Sediment from this "mud stream"

The quiet waters of Bayou Lafourche reflect a hazy winter sky. Once a main channel of the Mississippi River, the bayou today flows slowly past farming and fishing communities, sugar cane fields, marshland, and an oilfield service center before reaching the Gulf of Mexico.

settled along the coast of southwest Louisiana and southeast Texas, eventually forming the marshes of the Chenier Plain.

Because the Mississippi provided most of the mud for marsh building here, sediment supply and marsh growth were greatest when the river's mouth was nearest the region, as it was when the river followed the course of today's Bayou Maringouin, Bayou Teche, or Bayou Lafourche. When the river's mouth was in an eastern delta (such as the St. Bernard or Plaquemines-Balize [Modern] delta) and was therefore distant from southwest Louisiana, less sediment reached its shores.

During these periods of decreased sediment supply, the erosive power of the Gulf's waves and tides tore at the mudflats of the western coast and piled up beaches of sand and shell along their edges. The beaches grew in height and width until the Mississippi shifted west again and sediment

Sand, whole and crushed shell, and the flowers of sea ox-eye (Borrichia frutescens), *a member of the sunflower family, crown the beach at Joseph Harbor in Rockefeller State Wildlife Refuge.*

reaching the region increased. When this occurred, new mudflats grew in front of the old beaches and, anchored by vegetation, isolated them like islands in the marsh.

These ancient beaches remain today as chenier ridges. Because they mark the location of former shorelines, their age increases with increasing distance from the Gulf.

Since the 1950s, geologists have worked to determine precise ages for the ridges, as well as their correlation to the Mississippi's shifting deltas. All agree that the problem is complex. According to the most comprehensive study, the region's earliest ridges have subsided beneath the marsh, but five later ridge systems remain. These include Little Chenier–Little Pecan Island (ca. 2800 B.P.), Creole back ridge–Chenier Perdue (ca. 2500 B.P.), Smith Ridge–Creole front ridge–Pumpkin Ridge (ca. 2100 B.P.), Blue Buck Ridge–Cameron front ridge–Oak Grove–Grand Chenier–Pecan Island (ca. 1200 B.P.), and Mulberry Island–Cheniere-au-Tigre (ca. 600 B.P.).

It is not surprising that Louisiana Highway 82, the main east-west road across the region, follows the cheniers of the 1,200-year shoreline. These young ridges remain relatively high and broad, rising ten feet above

An east-west line of live oaks rises from the marsh, marking the location of a chenier. The oaks' dark green leaves and broad canopies make them easily recognizable, especially in winter when other broadleaf trees are bare.

Louisiana Highway 82 perches atop the "high land" of chenier ridges for much of its east-west course. Near the eastern end of Grand Chenier, live oaks draped in Spanish moss flank the road on each side.

the surrounding marsh and extending up to a quarter mile in width. They, along with neighboring cheniers, are reminders of the coast's dynamic origins rooted in the shifting deltas of the Mississippi River.

The River Today

The Mississippi no longer shifts its delta, and it no longer builds much land in south Louisiana. Most of the millions of tons of sediment it carries to its mouth each day slide into the deep waters off the edge of the Continental Shelf, for the delta has reached its farthest extent. The shorter, steeper route to the Gulf via the Atchafalaya's channel beckons, but the river has not shifted course. Why?

The river has followed its present route for approximately one thousand years. During this time, European settlers arrived, the United States became a nation and expanded west-

ward, and a river-based transportation and commercial infrastructure
developed. This nationally important
infrastructure would not have been
possible without the parallel development of techniques to aid people in
adapting to the Mississippi's floods
and meanderings.

Since the early twentieth century,
the U.S. Army Corps of Engineers
has borne responsibility for protecting riverside residents, businesses,
and industries from flooding. The
agency is also responsible for main-
taining navigation on this vital waterway. The corps' engineers have
addressed these challenges in two
ways. Today a network of levees
(raised earthen banks) and spillways
or floodways (land set aside as reser-
voirs for floodwaters) lines the Mississippi River from Cairo, Illinois, to
the river's passes. In addition, a massive water control structure keeps
the lower river on its present course
by limiting the amount of water that
flows from the Mississippi into the
Atchafalaya.

Levees, spillways, and water
control structures have been largely
successful in harnessing the restless
Mississippi River—to the economic
benefit of the nation, as well as many
generations of Louisianians. Unfortunately, these engineering successes
have also had a negative impact on
the state's coast, for they have halted
the natural processes of land build-

ing that created this special region of
wetlands and uplands over the past
seven millennia.

The Coast Today

Because the Mississippi's natural
land-building process has virtually
ceased, the heavy sediments of its
five deltas are compacting and sinking more rapidly, fraying the Deltaic
Plain into a ragged outline of myriad
ponds, lakes, and bays. The older
deltas, of course, have been slowly
subsiding since the river shifted away
from their areas to build new land
elsewhere. Since the 1930s, however,
human activities have accelerated
subsidence and land loss through
sediment deprivation, saltwater intrusion, and hydrocarbon extraction.

Today, high levees line the banks
of the Mississippi and prevent the
annual flow of freshwater, soil, and
nutrients across the land. Thousands
of miles of canals for navigation and
oil- and gas-well access pierce the
wetlands, providing conduits for saltwater to invade previously freshwater
areas. Spoil banks associated with
these canals alter the natural flow of
water through the marsh and swamp.
According to the Coalition to Restore
Coastal Louisiana's report *No Time to
Lose,* the state has lost more than one
million acres of its coast since 1930.
Each year another 24 square miles of

The Mississippi River levee system protects rural and urban areas from flooding. This view in June from atop the levee in St. James Parish, between New Orleans and Baton Rouge, shows the river level to be much higher than the land below.

coastal Louisiana sinks beneath the Gulf, and much of this loss occurs in the Deltaic Plain.

The Chenier Plain also experiences land loss as interior marshes, stressed by intruding saltwater, release their hold on the land and slowly convert to open water. Subsidence and land loss rates here, however, are lower than in the Deltaic Plain, for the finer clay sediments that underlie this region are less thick and cling together better than their deltaic counterparts. The Chenier Plain's shoreline, accordingly, appears smoother and less frayed than that of the neighboring region, although it still faces erosion

from the action of Gulf waves and sediment starvation.

A reader at this point might wonder whether there is much left to see of coastal Louisiana. Fortunately, the answer is an emphatic "yes." Some six thousand square miles of wetland and upland remain, including some of the largest expanses of marsh and swamp on the continent. Twenty-five percent of the United States' coastal wetlands, with 40 percent of the lower forty-eight states' salt marshes, lie in Louisiana. These coastal lands and waters provide habitats for a variety of plants and animals, as well as for people. Accordingly, both Deltaic Plain and

Development clings to a narrow strip of land along Bayou Terrebonne near Pointe-aux-Chenes. Subsidence and saltwater intrusion have taken their toll on the surrounding marshland and threaten the future of this community and other low-lying settlements. Courtesy of U.S. Army Corps of Engineers, New Orleans District.

Chenier Plain offer striking physical and cultural landscapes to explore.

A Naturalist's Trek

A traveler exploring Louisiana's two coastal regions at ground level encounters towns and rural communities, as well as uninhabited areas. This book focuses primarily on the latter, but it is wise to remember that, while some of these uninhabited landscapes may seem quite "natural," all have been shaped or influenced by people. Their activities over the years have included harvesting timber, moss, wildlife, fish, and shellfish; exploring for and extracting oil and natural gas; dredging canals and constructing roads, each with associated spoil banks; laying pipelines; introducing exotic species of plants and animals; and building a variety of structures to control water movement. These activities have transformed purely natural landscapes into "cultural landscapes" of human use and influence. Even the uninhabited coastal areas remind us that land and people are inherently intertwined.

In the Deltaic Plain, one such area is the Barataria Preserve of Jean Lafitte National Historical Park. Only

thirty minutes' drive south of New Orleans, this protected land is an oasis
amid the metropolitan area's urban
sprawl. The preserve of levee forest,
swamp, and marsh stretches along
the banks of Bayou des Familles, an
old Mississippi River distributary
that formed the western part of the
St. Bernard–Barataria delta some
two thousand years ago. The main
road, Louisiana Highway 45, follows
the banks of this bayou, and here
prehistoric Native Americans and
eighteenth-century Isleños (Spanish-speaking settlers from the Canary
Islands) lived. Today it is possible
to travel that road south from New
Orleans, away from the Mississippi's
banks, and explore the Deltaic Plain's
wetland habitats on the park's impressive network of boardwalk trails.

The Bayou Coquille Trail follows
the route of an abandoned oilfield
service road that once allowed access
to a well site deep in the wetland;
along it a visitor can walk from the
higher land of the bayou's natural
levee into land of lower and lower
elevation. The elevation change is
subtle, however, and what reveals it
is not the visual perception of a slope
but rather the change in vegetation.
Here the naturalist's skills of observation come to the fore.

At the start of the trail near Loui-

*Loss of interior marshes accounts for much
of the wetland loss in the Chenier Plain. As
the land subsides and canals carry saltwater
inland, ponds become lakes and lakes join
together, increasing the ratio of open water
to vegetated marsh. Courtesy of U.S. Army
Corps of Engineers, New Orleans District.*

A walk through Barataria's hardwood forest is both shady and picturesque. Spanish moss (Tillandsia usneoides) grows in abundance; it was once harvested, dried, stripped of its gray outer coating, and used to stuff mattresses, upholstered furniture, and automobile seats. An epiphyte and member of the pineapple family, the moss uses the trees for support but does not draw nourishment from them.

siana Highway 45, a hardwood forest of live oak, water oak, and hackberry clings to the narrow strip of the natural levee. The trailhead is also the place where Bayou Coquille meets Bayou des Familles; here middens of clam shells, evidence of a staple in the Native Americans' diet, dot the levee and give the place its name, for *coquille* is French for "shell." Within a few feet of the bayou's banks, however, the forest includes swamp red maples and palmettos, indicating that the area is slightly lower and experiences occasional flooding. As Bayou

Coquille curves away, the land along the trail sinks another few centimeters, the oaks disappear, and a forest of baldcypress and water tupelo trees emerges from dark, clear water.

The presence of a trail has transformed many people's perceptions of the Barataria swamp from a forbidding place to one of beauty. Although biting insects abound in summer, so do butterflies and dragonflies. Gray cascades of Spanish moss drape the trees, and the purple-blue flowers of native giant blue iris emerge to color the swamp in spring. Water tinted brown by tannin from decaying leaves stands among the tupelos' flared bases and the cypresses' buttressed trunks and projecting aerial roots or "knees." Small fish and turtles swim around them, beneath tiny green spots of native duckweed. Alligators, snakes, birds, and furred mammals feed and rest here and are often visible at close range, to the naturalist's delight. With a trail to walk along, visitors need not worry about getting lost in the swamp, and it is easy to keep one's feet dry.

Along the trail, the careful observer notes that the Barataria swamp, while beautiful, is not pristine. Exotic water hyacinth and common salvinia flourish, and the furred mammal one sees most often is a South American species, the nutria.

The trees also indicate that humans have been at work here, for they are not the ancient giants of Audubon's day. Those fell to timber harvesters in the late nineteenth and early twentieth centuries; today only a few old cypress trees, ravaged by lightning and rejected by loggers, stand above their more slender progeny.

One of these ancient trees stands just east of the trail, in an area where the swamp becomes more open in appearance. The presence of fewer trees is the result of declining elevation, for here water stands on the land continually, preventing cypress seeds from

Barataria's cypress-tupelo swamp in April is a mosaic of greens, punctuated by the flowers of giant blue iris and, at left, the red stems and bright new leaves of swamp red maple (Acer drummondii).

The nutria, a rodent introduced to Louisiana from South America in the late 1930s, is common in the state's southeastern wetlands. Harvested for its fur for half a century, the species has proliferated as trapping has declined.

germinating. While the present trees will grow in inundated soil, no new trees will replace them when they fall. Accordingly, the swamp opens to vistas of marsh grass as the trail continues its imperceptible slide southward.

The boardwalk ends where the freshwater marsh meets the Kenta Canal, a long straight waterway that once carried the swamp's virgin timber to market. Some of these ancient logs sank along the way, and park service personnel have raised and laid a few of the "sinkers" at the canal's intersection with Bayou Coquille. The trail continues toward that bayou along the Kenta Canal's spoil bank, a narrow strip of raised land shaded

with exotic Chinese tallow, a fast-growing, invasive tree that is prevalent on spoil banks coastwide. A few native trees, along with shrubs such as wax myrtle, also cling to the low ridge that separates canal and marsh.

As the trail nears its end, a bridge across the Kenta Canal treats the naturalist to two impressive vistas. To the north is the tall, gleaming office tower of One Shell Square in downtown New Orleans, a reminder of the park's proximity to the metropolitan area. To the west is one of the world's largest expanses of *flotant,* a floating freshwater marsh growing atop thick layers of peat. Foot travel through the marsh ends here, as does the trail. With an airboat, it would be possible to skim across the marsh to Lake Salvador, switch to a flatboat or larger vessel, and journey south toward Barataria Bay and Grand Isle, the state's only inhabited barrier island. Today's visiting naturalists, however, are more likely to travel by car and so retrace their steps through marsh, swamp, hardwood forest, and eventually back to the Mississippi's banks, where roads to other parts of the coast await.

Although there is much more of the Deltaic Plain to explore, the naturalist's trek resumes in southwest Louisiana, where the Creole Nature Trail leads visitors to the marshes, ridges, wildlife refuges, and com-

munities of the Chenier Plain. There is no more impressive introduction to this region than a drive along the eastern part of the trail, from Lake Charles south to the Gulf via Louisiana Highway 27 and the Gibbstown Bridge.

On the way to the bridge, the naturalist passes through rice fields and pasture lands that today characterize the uplands of the Pleistocene Prairie Terrace, which borders the Chenier Plain to the north. Before immigrants from the Midwest brought mechanized rice cultivation techniques that transformed the area in the late nineteenth century, these clay uplands supported tallgrass prairies and associated wildlife, including prairie

Baldcypress trees give way to marsh grasses as the land gradually becomes lower in elevation and the soil remains saturated throughout the year. Raptors such as red-tailed hawks and red-shouldered hawks, common birds of prey at Barataria, often perch in these tall cypress trees at the marsh edge.

The Kenta Canal points north toward the city of New Orleans, reminding visitors of the link between urban development and natural resource source areas like Barataria. Trees grow alongside the canal because its spoil banks provide land of slightly higher elevation; beyond the trees and out of view is the marsh.

chickens and whooping cranes. Small areas of this former prairie are being restored on privately owned lands and at Cameron Prairie National Wildlife Refuge, which lies at the junction of the prairie terrace and the freshwater marsh.

Just south of the refuge visitor center, the Gibbstown Bridge rises high above the flat landscape. From its apex, the southbound traveler views a different world: a world of water and wetland. The Gulf Intra-coastal Waterway, a wide canal that carries barge traffic within the shelter of the wetlands, lies below. A marsh dotted with white water lilies and

American lotus extends east and west, and to the south the marsh grass stretches to a distant horizon marked by a dark line of oak trees. This world is the Chenier Plain, and a trip along Highway 27 is a trip through seven thousand years of coastal history. The farther one travels toward the Gulf, the younger the land becomes.

The old marsh of water lilies and lotus just south of the bridge is a deep freshwater marsh, and the common plants are floating aquatics. The water is two to four feet deep here not only because the marsh substrate has subsided over the millennia but also because a lengthy fire burned the marsh well into the peat layer during the early twentieth century. Accordingly, this area is known locally as the Big Burn. Its relatively deep water and abundance of vegetation harbor bass and other freshwater species, making the Big Burn a popular fishing destination.

As the naturalist proceeds south across the Big Burn, the vegetation changes. Shallower water allows emergent vegetation such as the broad-leaved plant bulltongue to establish roots in the saturated marsh soil and extend its leaves up through the water and into the air. Most of the Chenier Plain's common marsh plants fall into the category of emergent vegetation; among them are a variety of grasses, sedges, and rushes. In addition to bulltongue, stands of dark green bullwhip, aptly named for its slender whiplike blades capped with sharp tips, rise above the water. Beyond these marsh plants, a line of oaks becomes increasingly prominent, signaling the presence of a chenier.

Little Chenier ridge marks the 2,800-year shoreline in the central Chenier Plain. It is the first of four relict beaches that Highway 27 crosses on its way to the Gulf. Between Little Chenier, Creole back ridge and front

Cultivated rice (Oryza sativa) *flourishes in standing water, a strategy that reduces the growth of weeds. The clay soils of the prairie terrace north of the Chenier Plain hold water well, allowing farmers to irrigate their rice crops. Following harvest, cattle graze the fields for two years and replenish the soil's fertility with their droppings.*

A common moorhen (Gallinula chloropus) *swims among white water lilies in the Big Burn marsh south of the Gibbstown Bridge.*

ridge, and Oak Grove ridge lie additional marshlands. At Oak Grove, where the road meets Louisiana Highway 82 and turns to parallel the coast, yet another marsh stretches toward the Gulf. Its vegetation and appearance differ from those of the freshwater wetlands to the north, for it receives some of the Gulf's salty water and so is dominated by brackish marsh plants like wiregrass and leafy three-square. The road to Rutherford Beach lies just west of the Highway 27/82 junction and passes through this marsh, which is dotted with ponds alive with activity both above and below the water's surface. Gulls and terns skim and dive for small

fish, crustaceans, and insects, while people harvest crabs and larger fish, mimicking the herons and egrets that share their roadside perches.

The marsh ends at Rutherford Beach, which marks the present shoreline and is a good place to examine what is perhaps a chenier in the making. Here the naturalist's feet sink into sand and crushed shell, for in this period of low sediment influx from the Mississippi River, the Gulf's waves have taken charge and piled a broad beach at land's end. The sand is not pure white, however, for enough of the Mississippi's silt reaches these shores to tint the beach a light tan-brown hue. Amid the sand and shell

A small live oak rests precariously at the edge of a chenier ridge, while across the marsh a long line of oaks indicates the presence of another chenier.

Brackish marshes lie between the salt marshes nearer the Gulf and the freshwater and intermediate wetlands farther inland. One of the most common species of the brackish marsh is wiregrass, also known as marshhay cordgrass or saltmeadow cordgrass. Its slender leaves and stems bend readily in the wind and give these wetlands a distinctive, sculptured appearance.

Small houses or "camps" on the Louisiana coast afford owners and their guests opportunities for relaxation, recreation, and an escape from the routine of urban life and work. Hurricanes, however, are inescapable; these camps at Holly Beach, like those at Rutherford Beach, were washed away by Hurricane Rita's storm surge in 2005.

are round holes—burrows that house pale ghost crabs—and toward the beach's landward side rise low dunes stabilized by salt-tolerant vegetation, including exotic tamarisk or salt cedar.

Because Rutherford Beach is a popular spot for surf fishing, swimming, and beachcombing, its landward side also sports several streets that, prior to Hurricane Rita, were lined with raised houses or "camps." While outsiders may have scoffed at the small size and unpretentious na-

ture of these dwellings, camp owners, seasoned by hurricanes and tropical storms, knew the folly of building more substantial structures. The rebuilding period will likely demonstrate similar structural adaptations to living in a vulnerable region.

The visiting naturalist, however, is not thinking of storms but rather of the many species of life present in the Deltaic Plain and Chenier Plain. The field guide now turns to examine some of the common flora and fauna of these two coastal regions.

CHAPTER 3

Coastal Vistas

Vegetation

THE LOUISIANA COAST is characterized by a variety of wetlands and adjacent upland areas, and this chapter describes and illustrates some of their more common and easily observable plant species. The chapter emphasizes wetland plants, for it is the state's extensive swamps and marshes that make the Louisiana coast distinctive both physically and culturally. Without the wetland plants, which have adapted to an area's elevation, water depth, and water salinity—all of which are subject to change over time—a wetland would not be a wetland; it would be a body of open water.

The wetland plants are critically important for the coastal region's productivity, as well as for its long-term survival. These two stories are as intertwined as the myriad twisted roots of the wetland plants, for the roots not only supply nutrients, they also grip the wet soil, holding it in place and providing a matrix for the plants' continued growth. In the humid subtropical climate of south Louisiana, this growth is vigorous, and there is an abundance of both living and decaying plant material (detritus) in the wetland's shallow waters. While seeds, roots, and stalks of wetland plants nourish creatures like ducks, geese, nutria, and muskrats, detritus sustains organisms at the base of the food chain and feeds a multitude of fish and crustaceans. These include blue crabs, crawfish, brown shrimp and white shrimp, speckled trout, redfish, menhaden, largemouth bass, and many other aquatic species.

The brackish marsh, where fresh and saltwater meet, is an especially productive habitat that harbors post-larval and juvenile forms of many commercially and recreationally valuable fish and shellfish species. Its sheltered, food-rich waters provide a vital "nursery ground" for these tiny fish and crustaceans as they grow to adulthood. Without the roots of the plants to hold the soil in place against the erosive power of wind, wave, and tide, there would be no "nursery

ground," no wetland-based seafood
industry, no wild Louisiana seafood
in restaurants and family kitchens,
and no commercial and recreational
activity associated with the wetland's
wildlife and fishery resources. Economy and culture, as well as a sense of
coastal identity, are rooted in these
wetlands; they are as inseparable
from it as are the plants themselves.

Plant Distribution and Identification

The distribution of these plants tells
much about the lands and waters in
which they grow. How deep is the
water? Is it fresh or saline? Is this
"dry land" sometimes inundated, or
is it consistently well drained? The
photographs that constitute this part
of the guide help answer these questions. To facilitate identification, the
photographs are organized as typical
landscape scenes within four broad
and easily recognizable habitat types:
coastal uplands and wetland edges,
forested wetlands (swamps), grassy
wetlands (marshes), and beaches and
tidal mudflats.

Within these habitat types, the
photos depict common and easily observable plants in the context of their
surrounding species, and seasonal
vistas depict the species that are most
prominent or visible at a particular
time of year. The accompanying de-

scriptions are not the technical, jar-
gon-rich entries of a traditional field
guide; they are more observation ori-
ented and are designed to assist the
observer both with identification and
with learning more about the coastal
habitat in which the plants grow.
Readers will find additional information and additional species in the
books listed at the end of this work.

Coastal Uplands and Wetland Edges: Natural Levees, Cheniers, Barrier Islands, Spoil Banks, and Roadsides Adjacent to Wetlands

The "high lands" of coastal Louisiana
include natural levees along alluvial
rivers and bayous, chenier ridges,
and barrier islands, as well as hu-
man-made spoil banks and roadbeds.
These linear features provide habitat
variety in the coastal region, for their
elevations are several feet higher
than the surrounding wetlands, and,
accordingly, their soils are better

*Even a few inches of elevation makes a dif-
ference in determining what will grow in the
lowlands of coastal Louisiana. The large live
oak tree (Quercus virginiana) is rooted in
the slightly higher land of the chenier ridge,
while a decaying stump bears witness to the
fate of upland trees when their roots become
submerged. Photographed at Chenier Perdue
in November.*

The trunk of the honey locust tree (Gleditsia triacanthos) *features long, sharp spines, while its compound leaves (visible at upper left and upper right) are delicate arrangements of elliptical leaflets paired neatly on either side of the stem. The tree produces small white flowers in late March and early April; they attract insects, which in turn attract migratory birds hungry for a meal following their long trip across the Gulf of Mexico. Honey locusts bear their seeds in dark brown, foot-long pods that are usually evident beneath the tree. Photographed at Little Pecan Island in May.*

The 5-lobed, star-shaped leaves of sweet gum (Liquidambar styraciflua) *turn deep red in fall, adding color to the coastal uplands and wetland edges. Photographed at the Barataria Preserve in October.*

Beyond the shade of the oaks, a Canada goose (Branta canadensis) *lumbers through a springtime pasture ablaze with butterweed* (Senecio glabellus). *Contrary to what some might believe, the four seasons are clearly evident in the vegetation of coastal Louisiana. Photographed at Grand Chenier in April.*

The red-and-yellow flowers of Indian blanket (Gaillardia pulchella) *brighten the roadside during the plant's long blooming season, from April to December. Indian blanket grows in sandy and saline soils and is common near beaches as well as on cheniers and other coastal uplands. Photographed in eastern Orleans Parish near the Rigolets in May.*

(at left) Purple passionflower (Passiflora incarnata), *also called maypop, is a beautiful and distinctive plant of the coastal uplands. Its delicate lavender flower, three-lobed leaves, vine-like stems with tendrils, and round green fruit make it easy to recognize among other under-story plants. The Gulf fritillary, a common butterfly in the coastal region, uses passionflower as a host; it deposits its eggs on the underside of the leaves, which then feed the black-and-orange caterpillars that emerge. Photographed at Rockefeller Refuge in July.*

Honeybees (Apis sp.) *gather pollen from* spiny thistle (Cirsium horridulum), *an aptly named plant with a multitude of spiny leaves. This thistle grows from two to six feet tall and is common in idle fields and pastures and along roadsides. Hummingbirds hover over thistle flowers during migration, feeding on their nectar. Photographed at Rockefeller Refuge in March.*

Growing at the edge of a chenier is common mullein (Verbascum thapsus), *a plant of sandy soils and idle fields. From a rosette of leaves covered in soft, short hairs, a flower stalk ranging from six inches to three feet tall emerges. Its tightly packed yellow flowers bloom in summer and early fall. Some older chenier residents recall that the plant's leaves were smoked as a treatment for asthma. Flanking the mullein are two additional species of note: To the left is the leguminous shrub rattlebox* (Sesbania drummondii), *and to the right, the distinctive narrow leaves of southern cattail* (Typha domingensis). *Photographed at Little Chenier in October.*

Wooly rose mallow's large white flowers with deep red centers are a clue to its identity as a hibiscus species (Hibiscus lasiocarpos). *This shrubby plant, which grows from three to five feet tall, flourishes in wet soils, including those of wetland edges. It blooms throughout the summer. Photographed at Rockefeller Refuge in June.*

Tufts of eastern blue-eyed grass (Sisyrinchium atlanticum) *dot the coastal uplands and wetland edges in spring. While the flowers are small—approximately a half inch in diameter—their number and striking color make the plant easy to spot. Blue-eyed grass is a member of the iris family. Photographed at Grand Chenier in April.*

Roseau (Phragmites australis, *formerly* Phragmites communis), *a tall canelike grass of wetland edges and elevated sites in the marsh, sways easily in the wind. The large, plumelike inflorescence (flowering parts that produce the plant's seeds) develops in fall. Also known as common reed, roseau grows to heights of eight to twelve feet; it often borders roads that traverse marsh areas and is a favorite plant for covering duck-hunting blinds. Photographed in Vermilion Parish near Pecan Island in November.*

Spiderlily (Hymenocallis caroliniana) *blooms in spring in the moist soil of wetland edges, including spoil banks and other elevated sites in freshwater and intermediate wetlands. Identical white sepals and petals unite to form its central tubular flower. Swamp lily (Crinum americanum), a closely related member of the amaryllis family, grows in similar habitats but lacks this tubular flower structure. Photographed near Little Chenier in April.*

drained. Major storms may cause inundation, but the coastal uplands drain quickly as the storms recede.

These lands, well watered by an average of fifty-five to sixty inches of rain annually, support a variety of trees, shrubs, vines, grasses, and wildflowers. As the high lands gradually recede in elevation, more of this rainfall remains in the soil's upper levels, and the vegetation subtly changes to include species that are more water tolerant. This creates a transitional zone that I refer to as the "wetland edge"; this transitional zone may border either forested wetlands (swamps) or grassy wetlands (marshes).

Forested Wetlands: Swamps

A swamp and a marsh are not the same. Although people sometimes use these words interchangeably, this is technically incorrect. A swamp is a forested wetland, characterized by the natural growth of trees. A marsh is a grassy wetland, characterized by the presence of a variety of emergent grasses and sedges (those that rise above the surface of the water),

Baldcypress (Taxodium distichum), *a characteristic swamp tree, has a buttressed base for added stability in the relatively soft soil of the freshwater wetland. Surrounding the trunk are cypress "knees," roots that project above the water's surface. Dendrologists believe that the knees assist with stability, trap sediments around the tree's base, and absorb oxygen into the root system. Century-old baldcypress has insect-resistant properties and is a historically important building material. Behind the large cypress trunk at right is a palmetto* (Sabal minor), *distinguished by its fanlike arrangement of sharp, pointed leaves. The myriad tiny green plants coloring the water's surface are common duckweed* (Lemna minor), *an important food for ducks, nutria, and other wildlife. Photographed at the Barataria Preserve in January.*

as well as floating and submerged aquatic plants.

What separates a swamp from a marsh, and what determines what will grow in each, is elevation. As the coastal uplands decline in elevation beyond the wetland edges, water remains on the land's surface for much of the year. Although the water is fresh, such poorly drained land presents difficulty for many plants, for the soil is waterlogged and oxygen deficient. Some species, however, have adapted to these conditions and flourish in the swamp, giving this water-land its characteristic appearance. In the subtropical latitudes of coastal Louisiana, baldcypress and water tupelo trees, draped with cascades of Spanish moss, produce the classic swamp landscape image.

Moving through the swamp into lower elevations produces another transitional zone, an area where the cypress trees thin and low grasses such as wiregrass produce a soft carpet beneath them. This more open swamp is the result of slightly deeper and more continual inundation of the land, a condition that prevents cypress seeds from germinating. As the old trees die and fall, no new trees replace them; accordingly, a more open appearance characterizes this transitional zone, which eventually opens fully to the grassy wetland of the marsh.

Coastal Louisiana's swamps are freshwater environments. Prolonged inundation with salt water will kill baldcypress trees and other characteristic vegetation. Gaunt, silvery forests of dead cypress bear witness to declining elevation and/or increasing salinity. They are a striking reminder of the ongoing process of land loss in the state's coastal region.

The giant blue iris (Iris giganticaerulea), *one of coastal Louisiana's most spectacular native wildflowers, blooms in spring in swamps and freshwater marshes. Its flowers range from deep purple to pale blue. Photographed at the Barataria Preserve in April.*

Water tupelo (Nyssa aquatica) *is another characteristic swamp tree; its swollen base and broad, smooth-edged leaves distinguish it from baldcypress, which has knees, buttresses, and a featherlike leaf structure. The lower sections of water tupelo provide a soft yet durable wood prized by decoy carvers. Photographed at the Barataria Preserve in March.*

Lizard's tail (Saururus cernuus) *blooms from April to July in cypress-tupelo swamps. Colonies of this herbaceous plant are common in shallow, shady areas. Photographed in the Big Woods, Little Pecan Island, in May.*

The floating rosettes of water lettuce (Pistia stratiotes) and the clumping discs of common salvinia (Salvinia minima) can become so numerous in freshwater areas that they cover the water in a thick mat that blocks the penetration of sunlight, depletes oxygen, and reduces or eliminates important submerged aquatic plants. While water lettuce is native, common salvinia is an introduced species imported for use in aquariums and water gardens. Photographed at Lacassine National Wildlife Refuge (NWR) in June.

Buttonbush (Cephalanthus occidentalis) *is a shrub or small tree that grows in swamps and freshwater marshes, sometimes emerging from water several feet deep. It blooms in summer, producing pincushion-like flowers approximately one inch in diameter. Ducks eat the plant's seeds, and wading birds like herons and egrets use buttonbush thickets for nesting. Photographed at Lacassine NWR in June.*

The lavender flowers and bright green leaves of water hyacinth (Eichhornia crassipes) are an attractive sight in freshwater wetlands throughout coastal Louisiana. Unfortunately, this introduced species reproduces rapidly and covers the water with dense mats that impede navigation and fishing, reduce sunlight penetration, and inhibit the growth of wildlife food plants beneath the water's surface. Photographed near Little Chenier in June.

Although most of the exotic Chinese tallow trees (Sapium sebiferum) *surrounding this pond have shed their autumn-red leaves, this dense stand of fourchette flowers is still blazing. Fourchette, French for "fork," is the local name for bur-marigold* (Bidens laevis), *a herbaceous plant that produces an abundance of sharp, forked seeds. These seeds pierce the skin of nutria, forming pustules and damaging the pelt. Photographed at Little Chenier in October.*

Fanwort (Cabomba caroliniana) *is a submerged aquatic plant with branched, fan-shaped leaves. Its small white flowers open just above the water's surface. Fanwort grows in freshwater wetland ponds and provides good cover for fish, frogs, and insects. Photographed at the White Lake Marsh in July.*

American lotus (Nelumbo lutea) *is a large, attractive freshwater plant with umbrella-like leaves one to two feet in diameter. In late spring and summer, the stands of lotus produce yellow flowers four to six inches wide on stems that rise one to three feet above the water's surface. The flat-topped pod that develops at the flower's center holds edible, acornlike seeds; some older residents recall roasting and eating these seeds of the "water chinquapin." Photographed near Little Chenier in June.*

Stands of American lotus were common in the Big Burn and other freshwater marsh areas of the Chenier Plain prior to Hurricane Rita. While the storm surge inundated these wetlands with salt water and stripped them of floating vegetation, lotus seeds have a hard coating and can remain dormant in the mud for many years, affording hope for recolonization. Photographed near Little Chenier in June.

White water lily (Nymphaea odorata) graces quiet ponds in freshwater wetlands. Its circular leaves are approximately two to six inches in diameter and are cleft at the base. Here a flower, leaves, and buds cluster beneath a branch of black willow (Salix nigra) stretching from an adjacent spoil bank. Photographed at the Big Burn Marsh in April.

White water lily blooms in spring and summer; the bloom can be spectacular when the lilies extend across large areas of the water's surface. Amid the lilies near the foreground is a taller, emergent plant, bulltongue. Photographed at the Big Burn Marsh in April.

Grassy Wetlands: Marshes

As land elevation declines to a point where water covers the surface of the land continually during most years, even water-tolerant trees like baldcypress and water tupelo cannot successfully reproduce. In these areas grasses and sedges predominate, and a marsh rises above the waterlogged soil. The marsh, though a wet grass-land, shares characteristics with other, drier grassland regions. The roots of its myriad grasses hold the soil in place, fortifying it against erosion. These roots also enrich the soil with nutrients, making it extremely productive.

In the humid subtropical climate of south Louisiana, a constant cycle of plant growth, death, and decay takes place in the marsh, enhancing the soil with a thick layer of organic material, in addition to its mineral components. Here the productive wet prairie nurtures and nourishes many life-forms, including commercially and recreationally valuable species of fish and shellfish and an abundance of birds, reptiles, and furbearing mammals.

The gentle gradient or slope of the land, along with a low tidal range (approximately one foot range between high and low tides), result in wide expanses of marsh through which fresh water that drains slowly southward very gradually mixes with the Gulf's salt water, resulting in four distinct marsh types. These marsh types are characterized by their water salinity, measured in units of parts per thousand (ppt). (For reference, seawater has a salt concentration of 36 ppt; 1,000 pounds of seawater contains 36 pounds of salt.) Coastal Louisiana's four marsh types are *freshwater marsh,* with negligible salinity of 0.5 to 1 ppt; *intermediate marsh,* with a low salt concentration of 3.3 ppt; *brackish marsh,* with higher

The roots of wetland plants hold the soil in place, enrich it with nutrients, and help neutralize toxins. They are the vital link that keeps the wetland healthy and productive. These roots belong to bulltongue, a member of the water plantain family; its extensive root network includes rhizomes that allow the plant to spread across large areas. Photographed at the Rainey Sanctuary, Vermilion Parish, in July.

Bulltongue (Sagittaria lancifolia) *is a common plant of freshwater and intermediate marshes. It grows in dense stands and can cover vast areas. Bulltongue's lance-shaped leaves are two to three feet tall; its small white flowers appear on stalks that rise above the leaves in spring, but plants occasionally bloom through summer and into fall. Photographed between Grand Chenier and Pecan Island in June.*

The tall, dark green stems of giant bulrush (Schoenoplectus californicus, *formerly* Scirpus californicus)—*locally known as bullwhip—bend in the breeze, weighted by effusive flower heads that will produce seeds for new plants and for wildlife. A sharp, hard bract extends two to three inches above the inflorescence, giving the plant its local name. While this sedge flourishes in freshwater and intermediate marshes, it is more common in the latter, where it grows four to eight feet high in dense, scattered stands. Photographed at Sabine NWR in May.*

Maidencane (Panicum hemitomon) *is a common freshwater marsh grass; it grows to heights of two to four feet in highly organic soils and can extend across large areas. In summer, maidencane marshes are bright green, but in winter the marsh blanches. As the old growth decomposes, it contributes organic matter for marsh building and nourishes life in the food web. Photographed at the White Lake Marsh in January.*

Cattails stand out among all other marsh vegetation. Broadleaf cattail (Typha latifolia), *a common species of freshwater and intermediate marshes, has a cylindrical, dark brown flower spike five to seven inches long and leaves four to six feet tall. Flower spikes form in spring and summer; by late fall and winter they become cottonlike as the seeds begin to disperse. Photographed at Rockefeller Refuge in June.*

The large, feathery inflorescence and sharp-edged leaves of giant cutgrass (Zizaniopsis mili-
acea) distinguish this freshwater marsh plant, which often grows in dense, circular stands.
The inflorescence is one to two feet long, and the seeds it produces provide food for wintering
ducks. Photographed at Rockefeller Refuge in May.

A soft carpet of wiregrass (Spartina patens) stretches beyond the taller vegetation in the
foreground, a stand of three-cornered grass, or Olney bulrush (Schoenoplectus america-
nus, formerly Scirpus olneyi). These species are common in brackish marshes, though wire-
grass grows in all marsh types and is considered one of the dominant plants of the coastal
wetlands. Photographed at Rockefeller Refuge in June.

The triangular stems of three-cornered grass rise from the wet mat of previous generations' growth. This constant cycle of growth, death, and decay of marsh vegetation provides detritus in abundance, along with organic matter that slowly builds land in the wetland. In addition, the brackish marsh is the base of the state's seafood industry, for its plants provide food and cover for myriad tiny fish, crabs, and shrimp as they grow to adulthood. Photographed at the Rainey Sanctuary in July.

Leafy three-square (Schoenoplectus robustus, *formerly* Scirpus maritimus [Scirpus robustus]), *also known as sturdy bulrush, is a sedge that flourishes in intermediate, brackish, and salt marshes. Its inflorescence is a distinctive cluster of brown, bristled spikelets, each approximately an inch long. Ducks feed on the seeds of leafy three-square, which often grows as scattered plants intermixed with other species. Photographed at the Rainey Sanctuary in July.*

Saltmarsh mallow (Kosteletzkya virginica) *flowers from late spring to early fall in fresh-water, intermediate, and brackish marshes. It grows on slightly elevated sites and reaches heights of two to three feet. Photographed at Sabine NWR in June.*

Salt matrimony vine (Lycium carolinianum), *a member of the nightshade family, grows in salt marshes and on slightly elevated adjacent sites. Also known as wolfberry, this woody shrub has succulent leaves and produces red fruits approximately a half inch in diameter. Three months after Hurricane Rita's storm surge, salt matrimony plants throughout Cameron Parish were laden with the bright red berries. Photographed near Johnson Bayou in November.*

Smooth cordgrass (Spartina alterniflora) *grows in dense stands over large areas in intermediate, brackish, and salt marshes. Its salt tolerance makes it a dominant species in the latter marsh type; it also flourishes on shorelines and barrier islands, where waves and tides frequently inundate it. Locally known as oyster grass, the plant has red-tinged stems that are thick and tightly packed, allowing it to buffer waves and collect sediment. Accordingly, this species is frequently used in marsh and beach restoration projects. Photographed east of Sabine Pass in January.*

Black mangrove (Avicennia germinans) *is an evergreen shrub with dark green leaves and an extensive root system; it grows in brackish and saline soils in the Deltaic Plain, primarily east of Atchafalaya Bay. It is sensitive to cold weather, and freezing temperatures may limit its distribution. Black mangrove thrives in salt marshes and other areas subject to tidal inundation, including barrier islands, where it provides nesting sites for brown pelicans and a variety of wading birds. Photographed south of Port Fourchon in April.*

salinity of 8 ppt; and *salt marsh,* with salinity of 16 ppt, nearly half that of seawater.

Plant distribution in the marsh is linked to both salinity and water depth. Deeper freshwater areas often support floating aquatic plants like American lotus and white water lily, while shallower freshwater areas may be nearly covered in maidencane, bulltongue, or cattails. As salinity increases slightly, other plants like bullwhip, a typical species of the intermediate marsh, become more prominent. As the water becomes more and more salty, fewer species can tolerate its harsh demands on plant tissue. Plant diversity thus decreases with increasing salinity, and a few characteristic species like wiregrass, black rush, leafy three-square, three-cornered grass, and oyster grass predominate in Louisiana's brackish and salt marshes.

Beaches and Tidal Mudflats

Beaches of sand and crushed shell, as well as dark tidal mudflats, mark the interface between Louisiana's vast wetlands and the Gulf of Mexico. The sand here is not glaring white but rather is a soft tan in color, tinted by the Mississippi River's muddy sediment, which flows westward with the longshore current. Subject to wind, salty waves, and inundation by storm tides, this is a harsh zone for vegetation. Plants that thrive here have adaptations for excreting salt or conserving water, such as waxy coat-

ings on their plump, succulent leaves. Though they may have a tenuous existence, beach and mudflat plants are nevertheless important, for their roots help anchor the sand and mud and keep barrier islands and other shore areas from shifting . . . at least for a time.

The shoreline zone has marked both the birth and death of land, for the state's coast is a dynamic one, growing in some areas while disappearing beneath the waves in others. The mudflats in Atchafalaya Bay, for example, herald the rise of a new delta that in time will support new

A variety of beach plants grow above the normal high tide line, trapping sand and anchoring the dunes. At left, the tall, bluish-green leaves of bitter panicum (Panicum amarum) *block the wind, while in the foreground, a goat-foot morning glory vine* (Ipomoea pes-caprae) *stretches across the sand. Chapter 2 includes a photo of sea ox-eye, another common beach species. Photographed at Peveto Beach in July.*

The seeds of smooth cordgrass germinate and take root on beaches and tidal mudflats, eventually providing some stability for the soils of these fragile, ever-changing environments. Photographed at Fourchon Beach in November.

Bigelow glasswort (Salicornia bigelovii) *is a succulent herbaceous plant with numerous jointed, branching stems. It grows on well-drained saline sites on beaches, pond and bayou banks, bay shores, and salt marshes. Photographed at Fourchon Beach in July.*

Goat-foot morning glory (Ipomoea pes-caprae) *has stems up to twenty feet long and can easily cover a dune. Its funnel-shaped purple flowers bloom from May to November among thick, nearly round leaves four to six inches long. A closely related species, beach morning glory* (Ipomoea imperati), *has a white flower with a yellow center; its leaves are half the size of its larger relative. Photographed at Fourchon Beach in October.*

Beach (Drummond's) evening primrose (Oenothera drummondii) *colors sandy sites with bright yellow flowers two to three inches in diameter. The flowers bloom from April into June, turning toward the sun each day on their short, fuzzy stems. Photographed at Rutherford Beach in May.*

marshes, while the sand and shell exposed beneath Peveto Woods Sanctuary, which lies adjacent to the Gulf in western Cameron Parish, attests to the erosion of a chenier ridge. Barrier islands such as Grand Isle in southeast Louisiana also erode and accrete, slowly shifting positions or "migrating." Severe storms can accelerate this migration, changing the map of coastal Louisiana in a matter of hours.

Humans have also influenced the shoreline's evolution. Mudflats east of Calcasieu Pass near Cameron bear witness to the sediment-blocking action of the jetties that flank the pass. These structures aid navigation but reduce sediment to more western areas of the coast such as Holly Beach and Constance Beach. Sand replenishment projects in this area and at Grand Isle in southeast Louisiana attempt to address this facet of the erosion problem, while plantings of salt-tolerant vegetation strive to hold the fragile land in place.

CHAPTER 4

Coastal Vistas

Wildlife

WILDLIFE ABOUNDS in Louisiana's coastal zone. As a visitor drives through or along the edge of the region's wetlands, however, only a small fraction of this abundance is evident. Muskrats, for example, are more active at night than during the daylight hours when visitors are afield. Alligators may be difficult to see on a cold, cloudy day. The myriad insects that thrive here often go unnoticed, except for butterflies, dragonflies, mosquitoes, and biting flies. Frog species that fill the evenings with their loud choruses are well camouflaged and difficult to spot when silent. A glimpse of aquatic life, too, requires a keen eye—or a fisherman eager to show off the day's catch.

Other types of wildlife are readily visible but are present in certain seasons and absent in others. More than twenty species of ducks and geese winter in Louisiana wetlands, but in summer only the mottled duck and wood duck, along with small numbers of blue-winged teal and Canada geese, are present. A variety of songbirds, shorebirds, and raptors (birds of prey) migrate through the region in spring and fall, but their number and diversity decline in summer and winter.

Fortunately, a number of large wading birds, including herons, egrets, ibises, and the spectacular roseate spoonbill, are present year-round and form the most visible group of wildlife in the state's coastal region. Along with the American alligator, these wading birds are closely associated in many visitors' minds with Louisiana wetlands, and a sighting of any of these "hallmark" creatures is a memorable and exciting experience that makes one's visit complete.

This chapter offers suggestions for safely and successfully viewing wetland wildlife and portrays some of the more common and easily observed species, including a variety of birds, several larger mammals, and some representative reptiles, insects, and aquatic creatures. Frogs and toads, amphibians abundant in the coastal zone but more difficult to see, highlight the section on audible wildlife. For those seeking more comprehensive coverage of the region's myriad species of birds, mammals, reptiles, fish, and insects, the works listed in the resource section at the end of the book offer additional illustrations and details.

Viewing Coastal Wildlife

Walking a refuge nature trail or driving or boating slowly through Louisiana's lowlands, a visitor will no doubt see wildlife with the unaided eye. Binoculars, however, offer additional opportunities to spot and observe creatures at a greater distance, which causes them less disturbance. In all cases, however, safety is paramount. To view wildlife from the road, drive to a spot where you can pull your vehicle safely *all the way off the road,* then, if necessary, walk back to the area of interest. Remember, too, that wild creatures are unpredictable; approaching or feeding them jeopardizes their wildness and your safety. Please enjoy them from a safe distance, and simply let them coexist in their natural setting.

While on foot, staying quiet along the trail will enhance your opportunities to observe wildlife and will allow you to focus on the sights and sounds of nature. Moving slowly and stopping frequently during your walk will also optimize your chances to see wild creatures and observe their behavior.

Towers and viewing blinds, present along some refuge trails, are excellent places to watch wildlife. Your vehicle can also serve as a viewing blind when you are safely off the road or driving slowly along a refuge auto tour route. "Slowly" is key in all cases, for wild creatures are vulnerable to collisions with vehicles, especially during the spring and summer breeding season, when young are present. I have found that when traveling at speeds of less than fifty miles per hour (on roads where this is possible), I have been able to avoid collisions with wetland wildlife; above fifty mph, it is difficult for me to dodge animals whose habitat the road traverses.

A final tip to enhance your wildlife viewing experience is a reminder that Louisiana's coast is a "working wetland," where land and people are intertwined in a culture that is highly inclusive of the land's bounty, including its wild creatures. As you travel the roads, you will be sharing them with residents on their way to and from work, running errands, and transporting children, friends, boats, and livestock. Please drive safely, and never stop in the roadway to view wildlife or take photographs, no matter how quiet or little traveled the road seems. Please also respect private property; never trespass, never litter. Be aware, too, that many federal and state refuges and sanctuary areas provide public access to wetlands, and some offer facilities such as visitor centers, nature trails, auto tour routes, and restrooms. Chapter 7 describes these excellent wildlife viewing locations, places that welcome visitors to experience Louisiana's coastal wetlands at a leisurely pace, the best pace for observing and enjoying the region's wild creatures.

Look and Listen

Sounds are among the many sensory gifts of Louisiana's coastal wetlands. The calls of nesting birds and their young in spring and summer, the bull-like bellowing of male alligators in May, and the "music" of ducks and geese in fall and winter enrich the coastal landscapes and remind us of their vitality. Among the most prolific singers of these lowlands, however, are the region's frogs and toads. Different species take up the chorus at different times of the year, and some sing in daylight hours, usually late afternoon and early evening, as well as after nightfall. Here are some of the common species a visitor will hear, along with a description of their calls and the time of year they are most

prominent. Additional information, including an excellent website that features recordings and photographs of these species, appears in the list of resources at the end of the book.

Spring peeper: high-pitched, emphatic peep; late fall through winter

Upland (southeastern) chorus frog: creaking call, like thumbing the teeth of a comb; winter

Southern leopard frog: low-pitched "chuckle," a tremulous "huhhuhhuhhuh"; winter

Northern cricket frog: rapid clicking; spring and summer

Cope's gray tree frog: short, high-pitched trill, like the sound of a police whistle; spring and summer (the similar but less common gray tree frog has a slower, lower-pitched trill)

Green tree frog: repetitive "ank" call; in chorus with others it sounds like a seesawing "hank," "thank," or "quank"; spring and summer (the squirrel tree frog has a similarly emphatic and repetitive "rank" call)

Gulf Coast (coastal plain) toad: prolonged, low-pitched rattling trill; spring and summer

Eastern narrow-mouthed toad: long, emphatic "baaaaaa" trill reminiscent of a bleating sheep; late spring through summer

Woodhouse's toad: fast, agitated

"WAAAA" or "RAAAA," trill reminiscent of a scream; spring and summer

Bronze (green) frog: distinctive "tunk," "tunk tunk," "tunk tunk tunk"; spring and summer

Pig frog: low-pitched grunts reminiscent of a pig's grunting, delivered in same rhythm as the bronze frog's call; summer

Bullfrog: distinctive low-pitched "wa wa roh," origin of the Louisiana Cajun French word for bullfrog, "ouaouaron"; summer

A Wildlife Portfolio

The following photographs present the coast's diverse wildlife in broad groups, beginning with birds and continuing with larger mammals, reptiles and amphibians, fish and shellfish, and insects. Additional examples appear in previous and subsequent chapters, where animals are part of illustrations that highlight vegetation or human activities. These examples remind us of the inseparability of wild animals and their habitat, as well as the interaction between people and wildlife that is a hallmark of the Louisiana coastal region.

An American white pelican (Pelecanus erythrorynchos) *swims in the winter marsh. Flocks of white pelicans grace the skies as well as the waters in winter; the birds often soar, their white bodies and black-edged wings tilting in unison. While white pelicans work together in small groups to catch fish, the darker brown pelican* (Pelecanus occidentalis) *dives for its quarry. Brown pelicans are resident year-round and nest on the barrier islands; once extirpated due to the egg-thinning effects of pesticides such as DDT, Louisiana's state bird has recovered but faces recurring challenges from hurricanes and land loss. Photographed east of Grand Chenier in January.*

A least bittern (Ixobrychus exilis) *clutches the branches of the shrub rattlebox, which retains several dried seed pods from the previous growing season and has some new leaves emerging. Least bitterns, the smallest of the region's herons, are present in summer; although they are more secretive than their relatives, they occasionally fly low over the marsh grass or perch briefly in open areas. Their bright, buff color and light streaks on the underside of the neck are good clues for identification. Photographed at Little Chenier in April.*

A great egret (Ardea alba) *stalks the shallows in search of food. The largest of several white wading birds common on the Louisiana coast throughout the year, the great egret has a long, slender neck, a yellow bill, long white back plumes, and black legs. Photographed at Sabine NWR in January.*

The snowy egret (Egretta thula) *is distinctive in its combination of small size, slender build, black bill and legs, and bright yellow feet. Once hunted for the beautiful white plumes that signify its readiness for breeding, the snowy egret, like other nongame birds, is now federally protected. This snowy egret is waiting atop a water control structure for small fish or crustaceans that may pass through or congregate at its gate. Photographed at Rockefeller Refuge in May.*

A tricolored heron (Egretta tricolor)*, formerly Louisiana heron, displays its breeding plumage. While its back and neck are primarily dark, the contrasting pattern on its underparts— thin neck stripe, dark breast, and white belly—distinguish it from other herons and egrets, even when it is in flight. Photographed near Grand Isle in June.*

This green heron (Butorides virescens), *a summer resident, has bright orange legs during the breeding season. To its left are the leaves of Chinese tallow, and below and to the right are the purple-blue flowers of pickerelweed* (Pontederia cordata), *a plant of freshwater wetlands. Photographed at Chenier Perdue in June.*

A roseate spoonbill (Ajaia ajaja) *in its summer breeding plumage stands in striking contrast to the green of the marsh. The spatula-like bill and distinctive rosy color give the bird its name. In fall and winter, however, roseate spoonbills become paler and can appear nearly white. Photographed west of Cameron in May.*

Amid the furrows of a harvested rice field, greater white-fronted geese (Anser albifrons) look for seeds in the stubble. These large birds with bright orange legs, pinkish bills, white feathering behind the bill, and dark markings below the breast are locally known as "specklebellies." Flocks are numerous in winter, when they sometimes feed among snow geese, another common wintering species (depicted in chapter 5). Photographed north of Lacassine NWR in December.

Mottled ducks (Anas fulvigula) cruise among a scattering of water hyacinths on a pond. While many duck species use these wetlands in fall and winter, mottled ducks remain in coastal Louisiana throughout the year. Both males and females have brown feathers with lighter edges, creating a patterned appearance; feathering on the head is a slightly lighter brown. Photographed at Little Chenier in June.

A pair of blue-winged teal (Anas discors) join two American coots (Fulica americana) in the intermediate marsh. The male blue-winged teal's face pattern—a bold white crescent—is unmistakable; the female's soft browns will camouflage her on the nest. Coots often use the same habitats as ducks as they dive in search of aquatic plants. Beyond the birds, on the bank behind and slightly to the left of the teal, an American alligator basks; though these reptiles are more active in spring, summer, and fall, a warm winter day may induce a gator to leave its den. Photographed at Sabine NWR in January.

A purple gallinule (Porphyrula martinica) strides across a mat of water hyacinths. While the gallinule's relative, the common moorhen (illustrated in chapter 2) is present all year, the purple gallinule is a summer resident only. Photographed at Lacassine NWR in June.

A variety of shorebird species winter in or migrate through coastal Louisiana. They feed and rest on beaches, barrier islands, mudflats, shallow marsh ponds, flooded rice fields, and bay edges. This flock of shorebirds includes a dowitcher (Limnodromus sp.), the stocky bird at far left with the long straight bill; to determine whether this is a long-billed or a short-billed dowitcher, it helps to hear the bird's call. In the foreground to the dowitcher's right is a shorter-billed bird, a pectoral sandpiper (Calidris melanotos), so named for the sharp demarcation between its dark, streaked breast and white belly. Photographed near Johnson Bayou in March.

Black-necked stilts (Himantopus mexicanus) pick insects and other small prey from shallow marsh ponds, mudflats, and flooded rice fields. Their black and white plumage and bright pink legs are distinctive. Black-necked stilts are present in coastal areas throughout the year. Photographed north of Grand Chenier in November.

Mixed flocks of gulls and terns are common on the state's beaches. Beneath a stormy spring sky, these common terns (Sterna hirundo) display their dark gray shoulder bar. While common terns migrate through the region, the much larger Caspian tern (Sterna caspia) at far right is a resident species. Its complete black cap and stout red bill distinguish it from the similar royal tern (Sterna maxima), which sports a white forehead and yellowish bill after the breeding season. Alone among the terns is a laughing gull (Larus atricilla), one of the most common gull species; this black-hooded bird is in breeding plumage. Photographed at Holly Beach in May.

Forster's tern (Sterna forsteri), a year-round coastal resident, lacks the dark shoulder bar of the common tern. This Forster's tern shows the full black cap, bicolored bill, and bright legs of a bird in breeding condition. In fall and winter its bill is black, and the cap is merely a dark smudge behind the eye. Photographed north of Rutherford Beach in March.

A graceful flier, the black skimmer (Rynchops niger) *is present throughout the year on Gulf beaches. Observers often see this bird flying parallel to the shore, the lower half of its bill "skimming" or cutting through the water's surface; when it makes contact with a small fish, the bill snaps shut, seizing its prey. Photographed at Rutherford Beach in July.*

Eastern kingbirds (Tyrannus tyrannus) *arrive early in spring and remain through the summer breeding season. A member of the family of tyrant flycatchers, eastern kingbirds perch in open areas and watch for flying insects, which they snatch from the air. The bird's dark head and back, light underparts, and black tail with white tip are easy to recognize; use caution when passing them on the roadways, as they sometimes sally out into traffic. Photographed at Rockefeller Refuge in May.*

A male common yellowthroat (Geothlypis trichas) finds concealment among stems of roseau. While many warbler species migrate through the region, the common yellow-throat is resident year-round and frequents marshes and other brushy areas near water. Only the male has the bold black mask; female and immature birds have a yellow throat and yellow feathers beneath the tail but are otherwise a light olive-brown. Photographed at Rockefeller Refuge in November.

The indigo bunting (Passerina cyanea) is one of many brightly colored songbird species that migrate through coastal Louisiana. This bird's worn plumage may be the result of disease, a late molt, a difficult Gulf crossing, or damage from the mist net in which it was trapped for research. Photographed at Grand Chenier in April.

A Baltimore oriole (Icterus galbula, *formerly northern oriole*) *feeds among the leaves of a honey locust tree in a Chenier Plain woodland. Stands of coastal forest on cheniers, natural levees, and barrier islands provide essential stopover habitat for a variety of neotropical migratory birds. Photographed at Peveto Woods in April.*

The nutria (Myocastor coypus), *a native of South America, was introduced to Louisiana's coastal wetlands in the late 1930s. This large, herbivorous rodent with orange teeth feeds on water hyacinth, duckweed, and many additional wetland plants, often consuming roots as well as leaves and stems. Coastal scientists believe that large numbers of nutria feeding in an area can accelerate damage to deteriorating marshes, hence a bounty payment entices trappers to reduce nutria populations. Photographed at Little Chenier in April.*

Because the common muskrat (Ondatra zibethicus) *is active at night, its presence in an area is apparent primarily by the numerous low mounds of vegetation in and under which it lives. These muskrat houses or muskrat "hills" are surrounded by shallow muddy water rather than marsh grass, indicating that an "eat-out" is well under way. Eat-outs occur when the native muskrats become too populous for their food supply. In brackish marshes, where they are most numerous, their preferred food is three-cornered grass (Olney bulrush). Photographed north of Rutherford Beach in February.*

A white-tailed deer (Odocoileus virginianus) bounds through the wiregrass toward a tall stand of roseau. To its left are cattails, and, in the right foreground, a few bulltongue plants emerge. Marsh-dwelling white-tailed deer have broader hooves than their dry-land counterparts, an adaptation that provides greater stability on soft, moist soil and matted vegetation. Photographed east of Grand Chenier in June.

*A swamp rabbit (*Sylvilagus aquaticus*) pauses while grazing near the edge of a chenier. Rarely far from the cover of vegetation, these common mammals are most active in late afternoon and early morning but may be seen any time of the day. Photographed at Little Pecan Island in May.*

*A biology student holds a young northern raccoon (*Procyon lotor*). The raccoon's familiar black mask makes it easy to recognize, whether it is on the ground or resting high in a tree. Because raccoons and other wildlife may bite and transmit disease, it is best not to approach or handle them. Photographed at Rockefeller Refuge in August.*

The American alligator (Alligator mississippiensis) *is a resident of swamps and freshwater, intermediate, and brackish marshes. Alligators often bask beside waterways on warm days in fall, winter, and spring, but in the heat of summer these reptiles are more frequently observed in the water. While alligators twelve to fourteen feet in length occur in coastal Louisiana, the statewide average size for gators harvested in the wild is seven feet. Photographed at Rockefeller Refuge in June.*

Is this a diamond-backed water snake (Nerodia rhombifera) *or a western cottonmouth* (Agkistrodon piscivorus)? *Both of these large, heavy snakes can reach lengths of five to six feet and frequently bask on branches above the water's surface. While the diamond-backed water snake is nonpoisonous, however, the western cottonmouth, often called water moccasin, is both venomous and aggressive. Additional differences include head shape (more flattened and triangular in most poisonous snakes) and markings: water snakes retain their distinctive coloring into adulthood, while cottonmouths tend to lose their banded pattern and become nearly black as they age. There is much variation among individuals, however, so it is best to maintain a safe distance from all snakes. Photographed at Cat Island Swamp in April.*

A speckled king snake (Lampropeltis getulus) *rests on a shell road following a kill. These nonpoisonous snakes are common residents of coastal uplands, where they consume a varied diet, including mice, rats, birds, snakes, and turtle eggs. Photographed at Little Chenier in July.*

The Gulf Coast ribbon snake (Thamnophis proximus orarius), *a subspecies of the western ribbon snake, is one of the most abundant snakes in coastal Louisiana. It is nonvenomous, inhabits both forested and open areas, and is seldom far from water. Photographed at Little Pecan Island in May.*

A green tree frog (Hyla cinerea) *perches atop a trailside bench in the Barataria swamp. Green tree frogs reach lengths of 2 to 2½ inches, have a distinctive light stripe on each side, and inhabit forested areas, pond and lake banks, and freshwater wetlands. This small amphibian's loud, repetitive call reminds some listeners of the dull ringing of a cowbell. Photographed at the Barataria Preserve in April.*

The southern leopard frog (Rana sphenocephala) *is well camouflaged for its life in a variety of habitats where fresh water is available, including swamps and freshwater marshes. Its dark spots and light yellow lines help careful observers distinguish it from the surrounding vegetation. At night, this four-inch-long frog gives a low-pitched, chuckling call. Photographed at Little Pecan Island in May.*

The red-eared slider (Trachemys scripta) *is the most abundant and widespread turtle of Louisiana's coastal wetlands. A red stripe behind each eye gives the turtle its common name, but many local people know it as the "yellowbelly" because of its yellow plastron (lower shell). These reptiles grow to lengths of eleven inches, and turtles of many sizes are often visible as they sun themselves on logs or beside waterways. This red-eared slider emerged from a pond to bask on a quiet road and still carries duckweed on its shell. Photographed at Rockefeller Refuge in June.*

A chenier resident holds a recently hatched red-eared slider and, above it, a common snapping turtle (Chelydra serpentina). *The snapping turtle, when young, is very similar to the alligator snapping turtle* (Macroclemys temminckii), *which grows to a larger adult size of 2½ to 3 feet and retains the three prominent rows of ridges or "keels" on its shell. While the common snapping turtle is a foot shorter in length, both species have large heads with very powerful jaws. Photographed at Little Chenier in July.*

As testimony to a successful summer of fishing, alligator gar (Lepisosteus spatula) *carcasses line a camp's fence. While not a choice food, this primitive fish of freshwater, intermediate, and brackish wetlands is edible; the soft white meat is molded into garfish balls or patties, seasoned, and fried. Photographed at Little Chenier in July.*

Although likely hoping to hook speckled trout and redfish (Cynoscion nebulosus *[spotted seatrout] and* Sciaenops ocellata *[red drum]*), *these fishermen have each landed a carp* (Cyprinus carpio), *an introduced fish that is common in fresh and brackish waterways. Photographed at Rockefeller Refuge in September.*

Blue crabs (Callinectes sapidus) *and brown shrimp* (Penaeus aztecus) *are among Louisiana's most valuable commercially and recreationally harvested shellfish species. In the hamper at left two upturned crabs reveal different shapes on the underside of their shells; the crab at top left with the thin, tapered basal segment is a male, while the crab at bottom right is a female. The female's broad basal segment can separate from the rest of the lower shell to reveal a spongy, yellow-orange egg mass. When female crabs are in this "berry stage," conscientious harvesters return them to the water so they can continue the reproductive process and increase the numbers of the next generation. Photographed at Lafitte in May.*

Soft, succulent meat lies within the shell of an American oyster (Crassostrea virginica) *pried from the reef and opened with a special shucking knife. Oysters are filter feeders and grow in brackish areas with water movement, including the lower part of estuaries and nearshore areas where a river or bayou meets the Gulf. Oyster harvesting begins in late fall, continues through the winter, and ends in spring. Photographed south of Grand Chenier in December.*

The red swamp crawfish (Procambarus clarkii) *is one of several freshwater crawfish species in the coastal region; it provides food for people as well as for many kinds of wildlife, including raccoons, a variety of wetland birds, and—in this case—fire ants* (Solenopsis sp.). *Wild crawfish, including those from the Atchafalaya Basin, are harvested in spring, while pond-raised crawfish are available nearly every month of the year. Photographed at Little Pecan Island in May.*

A viceroy (Limenitis archippus) *spreads its wings, displaying the dark, curving line on the hind wing that distinguishes it from the familiar but distasteful monarch* (Danaus plexippus), *which it mimics. Photographed at Rainey Sanctuary in July.*

A diagonal yellow band crosses the wings of the giant swallowtail (Papilio cresphontes), *the coastal region's largest butterfly. One of several swallowtails common in south Louisiana, this species has a wingspan of four to six inches. Photographed at Little Pecan Island in May.*

The Gulf fritillary (Agraulis vanillae) *is a bright orange butterfly with iridescent silver spots on its underwing. A familiar sight on the coastal uplands, especially in spring and fall, the Gulf fritillary lays its eggs on passionflower vine and takes nectar from a variety of flowering plants, including Brazilian verbena* (Verbena brasiliensis). *Photographed at Rockefeller Refuge in October.*

Although the black witch (Ascalapha odorata) *is not common on the Louisiana coast, there have been repeated sightings of this spectacular moth, which can be especially numerous following the passage of hurricanes and tropical storms. A native of the American tropics, the black witch has a wingspan up to seven inches and is the largest moth to occur north of Mexico; it regularly migrates through Texas, primarily in June and July. Photographed at Rockefeller Refuge in July.*

Two male eastern pondhawks (Erythemis simplicicollis) *perch on the trunk of a large live oak. This dragonfly is common around vegetated ponds and is one of many species of drag-onflies and damselflies in the coastal region. While males are a powdery blue, female eastern pondhawks are bright green with black markings. Photographed at Chenier Perdue in June.*

Forest tent caterpillars (Malacosoma disstria) feed on the leaves of broadleaf trees and are especially abundant in swamps where water tupelo, a favorite food, is present. Despite their name, these social caterpillars do not build tents; instead, they spin silken mats upon which they gather for molting and resting. Photographed at the Barataria Preserve in April.

CHAPTER 5

Coastal Vistas

Human Activities

FOR MANY PEOPLE—local residents and visitors, city and country dwellers—the coast's fertile blending of land and water is rest for the weary, excitement for the adventure seeker, food for the table, and balm for the soul. Human use of Louisiana's "working wetland" has for generations incorporated both the harvest and appreciation of wetland wildlife, as well as other resource-related activities like cattle ranching, oil and gas extraction, and water management. This chapter describes some of the more visible human activities of the coastal zone. It anticipates and answers questions like "what is that person doing?" "what is that thing used for?" and "why is this here?" It also offers insight into aspects of wetland culture that may be less evident to a traveler but are a part of everyday life for people who live and work along the coast.

Recreational activities include pastimes like fishing, hunting, birding, and nature photography that enrich the lives of area residents and attract visitors to the region. While participants do not seek financial gain for their efforts, these recreational activities nonetheless are an important part of local and regional economies, for participants may spend considerable sums for equipment, fuel, food, lodging, guiding, and additional services.

Commercial activities, of course, also benefit the area's economies and individuals and heavily influence the cultural landscapes of coastal Louisiana. Today these landscapes bear the imprint of human activities such as oil and gas exploration, production, and support services; waterborne commerce; cattle grazing; and wildlife and fisheries harvest.

In addition to recreational and commercial activities, research and conservation-related activities take place here, for the Louisiana coast is a valuable resource that scholars and scientists have long deemed worthy of study, protection, and proper stewardship. Protecting and caring for the coast are not easy, however, for these tasks involve reconciling the conflicting interests and viewpoints of a variety of wetland users.

All wetland activities—recreational, commercial, and research/conservation—have one thing in common: they are dependent on the presence of healthy wetlands. As coastal land loss takes its toll on wetland acreage, these activities, along with the economies and cultures linked to them, become as vulnerable as the soil, vegetation, and wildlife that constitute Louisiana's swamps and marshes. If the activities are to survive, so too must the habitats and resources on which they depend.

People, Wildlife, and Wetlands

The following photographs depict seasonal activities in the coastal wetlands and waters as they progress through spring, summer, fall, and winter. Many of these activities are linked to peoples' use of wildlife and are influenced by the growth cycle and movements of species. Year-round pursuits, including mineral extraction, livestock ranching, and wildlife management, follow the seasonal vistas. The photos conclude with some examples of watercraft that make coastal resources more accessible to recreational and commercial users.

In late winter and early spring, as the days lengthen and warm, crawfish emerge from their burrows and begin to grow. Rice and crawfish farmers accordingly set wire mesh traps in their fields, which they often flood after the rice harvest in order to attract waterfowl. A variety of other birds, including herons, egrets, ibises, and many shorebird species, also use these "agricultural wetlands." Here a great egret hunts among crawfish traps in a flooded rice field in Vermilion Parish.

As early as the 1700s, the Houma—a southeast Louisiana tribe of Native Americans—used the crawfish as its emblem. Today the crawfish image is displayed throughout the southern part of the state and serves as a symbol of Cajun and coastal culture and identity. This restaurant in Lake Arthur, just north of the Chenier Plain, advertises both its style of cooking and a featured item on its menu.

Observing birds brings pleasure to thousands of nature enthusiasts, many of whom come from other states and foreign countries to observe the spectacle of spring migration in coastal Louisiana. From mid-March through mid-May, as birds flow through the state's forests and wetlands on their way to northern breeding areas, many are in colorful plumage and stand out among the green of new leaves, including those surrounding live oaks on Little Pecan Island. Birders often return to the coast later in the year to observe fall migration and wintering waterfowl.

With its variety of flora, fauna, landscapes, and human activities, the coastal region presents photographers with myriad subjects. Here a pond of white water lilies attracts the lens of a springtime visitor.

People of all ages enjoy a fishing outing, and many anglers cast their line right from the roadside. While sometimes a solitary pursuit that affords participants a chance to quietly connect with the natural world, fishing can also be an opportunity for socializing, as these boys demonstrate on a summer afternoon near Chenier Perdue.

Throwing a cast net for shrimp during the brown shrimp and white shrimp seasons is a popular pastime. It takes much practice to throw the weighted net so that it flares open and encircles as much water as possible.

A menhaden boat docked near Cameron is part of a fleet of large fishing vessels that harvest Gulf menhaden (Brevoortia patronus), a small oily fish also known as pogy. The smaller, more maneuverable boat suspended at its side sets the purse seine, a large net that can surround a school of menhaden and trap it with a drawstringlike closure device. This fishery accounts for the largest volume of commercial landings in Louisiana; the harvest takes place from April to October, when adult menhaden leave the shelter of the marshes and form large schools in the open Gulf.

Signs advertising a variety of seafood for sale bear witness to the importance of the coastal wetlands and waters as a source of both food and income. Such signs were a common sight at dockside facilities prior to the hurricanes of 2005; they are beginning to reappear as the state's commercial fishing industry recovers from the devastation to its vessels and infrastructure.

Phillip Vincent worked the waters of the central Chenier Plain for many years. He was visibly pleased when he hoisted this trap, heavy with blue crabs, from the waters of Grand Lake.

Shrimp boats trawl in lakes, bays, and shallow Gulf waters during the inshore seasons for brown shrimp (May through July) and white shrimp (Penaeus setiferus) (mid-August through mid-December). The timing of the inshore seasons coincides with the exodus of adult shrimp from the bays and marshes to the open Gulf. The offshore harvest season for both species extends from May to December, when adults are plentiful in the Gulf's deeper waters. The birds that typically follow shrimp boats may indicate a good harvest, or they may be feasting on small fish and other "bycatch" tossed overboard by the boat's crew.

Seafood boils are a popular activity during the warmer months when shrimp, crabs, and crawfish are plentiful and relatively inexpensive. The boiling usually takes place outdoors using a large pot and a gas burner. The shellfish are first purged in salted tap water to remove impurities and are then placed in boiling water seasoned with salt, cayenne pepper, halved lemons, and a packaged "crab boil" mix for additional flavoring. Potatoes, ears of corn, and garlic cooked along with the seafood provide tasty side dishes for this protein-rich meal.

Crab boils, shrimp boils, and crawfish boils are as much about socializing with family and friends as they are about eating seafood. Newspaper is the table covering of choice at these informal and celebratory gatherings.

The welcome arrival of cooler weather signals the start of the fall festival season. Although festivals celebrating coastal resources and culture take place at other times of the year as well, many communities host these gatherings as summer harvest seasons for wildlife conclude and fall harvest seasons begin.

Early morning light grazes the marsh as a waterfowl hunter poles a pirogue past a set of decoys. Hunters eagerly await the start of teal season in September and "big duck" and goose season two months later. In addition to the waterfowl seasons, there are also seasons for hunting deer, squirrels, rabbits, and doves.

Concealment is an integral part of waterfowl hunting, as this hunter demonstrates. In addition to his dark hood, he is wearing camouflage clothing and stands in a blind surrounded by netting, roseau, and cattails.

(left) The wild alligator harvest occurs during the month of September and is carefully regulated by the Louisiana Department of Wildlife and Fisheries. Each gator, including this one boated by Martin Trahan, has an assigned tag that must be attached to its tail in order for the hide to be sold. Buyers also purchase alligator meat, which many restaurants now feature on their menus.

Signs advertising hunting-related services are testimony to the economic importance of waterfowl hunting to people in coastal communities. In addition to paying to have their birds cleaned, many visiting hunters will also rent camps, buy groceries and gas, and lease wetland areas for their hunts.

Although once a lucrative winter occupation and a storied part of Louisiana wetland culture, trapping is today practiced primarily for population control of furbearing mammals that can damage fragile wetlands. Here a young outdoorsman sets a trap along a well-worn trail in a Chenier Plain marsh.

(right) Against a backdrop of early morning fog, Brandon Hess holds a nutria that found its way into a trap. Because many furbearers feed at night, trappers check or "run" the traps shortly after sunrise.

(above) Marsh burning takes place in winter when there is a light north wind and when adequate standing water protects the plants' roots. The burning removes thick mats of dead vegetation and stimulates new growth, which will attract flocks of snow geese and feed grazing cattle. Tender new shoots will appear within days of a burn such as this one in the brackish marsh of the National Audubon Society's remote Paul J. Rainey Wildlife Sanctuary in Vermilion Parish.

During fall, winter, and early spring, cattle like these in Cameron Parish graze the firmer marshes, including salt and brackish habitats where hardy Spartina grasses anchor the soil and provide forage. In summer, hordes of mosquitoes and biting flies present problems for marsh-grazing cattle, so ranchers transport them northward to higher ground. In the distance, jack-up oil rigs await transport from Sabine Pass to the Gulf of Mexico.

Coastal Louisiana is home to a number of oilfield service centers and rig fabrication and repair facilities. When completed, this rig along the Calcasieu Ship Channel in Cameron will have all the equipment necessary to hoist and turn its pipe and drill bit, store and circulate drilling fluid or "mud," control pressure in the boring, remove cuttings from the drilling mud, and generate power for these tasks.

(left) Winter brings large flocks of snow geese (Chen caerulescens) to coastal Louisiana, where they feed in rice fields and marshes. Their distinctive calls herald their presence and are an audible sign of winter. Both the white and the dark color morphs are present in large numbers; the dark geese with bright white heads were once considered a separate species, the blue goose, but many coastal residents and goose hunters know them as "eagleheads."

Oilfield "Christmas trees" dot the coastal landscape. Each assemblage of valves sits atop a producing oil or gas well. The valves regulate pressure, control oil or gas flows to pipelines, and allow access to the well bore for further hydrocarbon recovery work.

Signs marking oil and gas pipeline crossings are a familiar sight in the wetlands, coastal uplands, and shoreline areas. The Louisiana Department of Natural Resources reports that nearly fifty thousand miles of pipelines are at work beneath the state's lands and waters, with the largest pipeline mileage located in the nineteen coastal parishes.

A large female alligator stands guard just behind her nest, a two-foot mound of wiregrass surrounded by a skirt of dark water. The white-and-orange stake at left marks the nest's location in the brackish marsh of Rockefeller State Wildlife Refuge, where biologists have conducted research on the species since the 1960s and have developed a sustainable-use management program that serves as a model for crocodilian conservation efforts worldwide.

These alligator eggs were gently removed from a nest for transport to incubation chambers on Rockefeller Refuge. The eggs have relatively narrow central white bands and are approximately seven days old. The bands reveal the age and location of the growing embryo, while the dark pencil mark on each egg indicates its orientation in the nest so the fragile embryo can remain upright. Both researchers and licensed alligator farmers harvest alligator eggs during the summer nesting period.

As part of Louisiana's Alligator Management Program, approximately 17 percent of farm-raised alligators hatched from eggs collected in the wild are returned to the state's marshes and swamps. Here, alligator expert Ted Joanen (retired research leader at Rockefeller Refuge) releases a four-foot-long gator into a marsh pond.

The pirogue is a flat-bottomed boat well suited for travel in marshes, swamps, and other shallow water areas. Approximately eight to ten feet long and a foot deep, the pirogue is pointed at both ends and is frequently propelled by a person standing near the stern, "poling" the craft forward with a long wooden pushpole.

This waterfront home near Bayou Barataria in Lafitte features a boathouse with a speedboat suspended above the water on a sling and, to its right, a Lafitte skiff, a locally designed workboat used for shrimping on inshore waters. The Lafitte skiff's broad "fantail" at the stern serves as a platform for the net as it is lowered into or hoisted from the water, while the canopy provides welcome shade and some protection from rain. The large box near the bow is useful for sorting the trawl's catch, which includes not only shrimp and crabs but also an occasional large fish, many small fish, jellyfish, and grass.

Airboats provide unparalleled access to interior marshes and make activities like the collection of alligator eggs feasible. An airplane propeller fitted to the stern drives the aluminum-hulled craft, and a protective wire-mesh cage shields the boat's driver and passengers. This boat and driver have returned from an alligator-egg-collecting trip in a bulltongue marsh; the metal cans protect the eggs and keep them warm.

Two neotropic cormorants (Phalacrocorax brasilianus) *perch on a dock across from a crew-boat under repair and, to its left, a much smaller flatboat on a trailer. While the crewboat is frequently used in the oilfields, the inexpensive flatboat is used for both work and pleasure and is ubiquitous in coastal Louisiana.*

The marsh buggy is a large, tracked vehicle used for heavy-duty work in the marsh. Above its tracks is a platform on which crews and equipment ride. These expensive vehicles are useful for oilfield work and wetland management operations. A prized piece of equipment, this marsh buggy has its own shed at the Rainey Sanctuary.

CHAPTER 6

Wetland Loss and Restoration

LOUISIANA'S COAST has always been a dynamic place, growing in response to sediment deposition and retreating as the forces of subsidence and erosion take their toll. Since 1930, however, coastal Louisiana has lost approximately 1,900–2,100 square miles of its land. As of the year 2000, subsidence and erosion continued to tear away at the shore and convert interior wetlands to open water at a rate of approximately 24 square miles per year, the equivalent of losing a football-field-sized area of land every thirty-eight minutes. In a single year—2005— hurricanes Katrina and Rita transformed an additional 217 square miles of marsh to open water, and it is uncertain whether these wetlands will recover. These and additional statistics from the Louisiana Department of Natural Resources and the U.S. Geological Survey reveal that, without further measures to protect and restore the state's wetlands, beaches, and barrier islands, the coast may lose another 500 square miles by the year 2050.

How did coastal land loss become so dominant over land gain, and what is being done to address this major challenge for the state and the nation? This chapter examines these two questions and illustrates some of the ways such coastal change—and the battle to reverse it—are visible to an observer of Louisiana's wetland and shoreline regions. For readers who seek additional information, the resource section at the end of the book lists websites that contain current information from the Louisiana Department of Natural Resources, the National Wetlands Research Center, the America's Wetland Campaign, the Coalition to Restore Coastal Louisiana, and the Barataria-Terrebonne National Estuary Program, along with several recent books on the state's coastal land loss challenge.

The Shrinking Coast

The official Department of Transportation map of the state of Louisiana, updated for the year 2000, depicts a

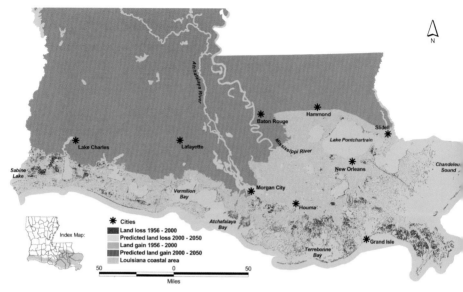

Estimates of land losses and gains in the coastal region from 1956 to 2050 reveal that more land is being lost than added to the state. Courtesy of U.S. Army Corps of Engineers, New Orleans District.

coast that looks much different from the one we have based our "mental maps" on for the previous fifty years. Throughout much of the Deltaic Plain, the new map reveals a coast that has receded toward the banks of the Mississippi River and the major bayous. Barrier islands have shrunk in size, and marshes that protect cities and smaller communities have become islands in a maze of open water. Only in the Atchafalaya Delta is land being added to the map. The Chenier Plain of southwest Louisiana has fared better, though its shoreline is receding in several places, and many of its interior marshes are dotted with large areas of open water.

There are many reasons for these startling changes. Some, like subsidence of old river deltas, are natural; they are simply part of a delta's evolution. Others, like construction of canals, ship channels, and levees, and the withdrawal of oil and gas, are related to human activity in and beyond the coast. Reality combines the two types of causes, natural and human, to produce the visible and measurable land loss evident in coastal Louisiana today.

Understanding the crisis begins, appropriately, with the Mississippi River, the land's creative force. The Mississippi, which built coastal Louisiana with its sediment, is now dumping much of its sediment load into a chasm, for the river has reached the "end of the line," the edge of the Continental Shelf. Confined by human-built levees (high earthen banks that border the river from Cairo, Illinois, nearly to the Gulf of Mexico) and kept on course by a major control structure, the Mississippi has not flooded the state's lowlands since 1927.

This, of course, has pleased and benefited those whose homes, businesses, industries, ports, and jobs lay within the river's vast floodplain. As we now know, however, control of the river has dealt a severe blow to the lands that protect and nourish those same people and their livelihoods, for the annual floods deposited fresh layers of sediment that compensated for the natural subsidence of the weighty delta. Today, there is no longer a balance of subsidence and sediment deposition in the coastal zone, and Louisiana is both sinking and shrinking as a result.

Adding to the ongoing challenge of subsidence is the problem of saltwater intrusion into areas of freshwater wetlands, a problem that the coastal region's numerous canals and navigation channels facilitate. Dredg-

The Mississippi River's passes form a classic "birdfoot" delta at its mouth. While land rises beside and delineates the passes, much of the river's sediment slides off the edge of the Continental Shelf. Courtesy of U.S. Army Corps of Engineers, New Orleans District.

The remains of a cypress forest in Bayou Sauvage National Wildlife Refuge in eastern Orleans Parish are grim testimony to the effects of saltwater intrusion. Courtesy of U.S. Army Corps of Engineers, New Orleans District.

ing transportation arteries through the marshes and swamps has over the years served the interests of logging, trapping, hunting, fishing, oil and gas extraction, and navigation, but, as with control of the Mississippi River, there has been a price to pay. These arteries frequently link the Gulf, brackish lakes, or bays with interior wetlands, providing a direct conduit for the movement of saline water much farther inland than would naturally occur. Saltwater intrusion into fresher areas kills vegetation and, as root systems disintegrate, land can easily wash away. Even canals in saline and brackish areas can contribute to land loss, for motorized boats create wakes that tear at the canal banks, eroding them over time.

Canals can also alter the wetland in another way. When a canal is dredged, the excavated soil is usually piled beside it, forming a spoil bank on one or both sides of the waterway. Spoil banks can impede or alter the natural flow of water through the wetland, changing its hydrology and impacting vegetation.

In addition to canal dredging, Mississippi River control, and subsidence of the river's deltas, more than half a century of oil and gas extraction has removed a tremendous volume of material from beneath the surface of the coastal zone. Geologists believe that this removal of material has resulted in deep faulting and accelerated subsidence in coastal Louisiana.

In today's energy-hungry world, oil and gas extraction will continue. Canals and navigation channels will remain to facilitate commerce and transportation. Flood control and port activities will still be top priorities along the Mississippi River. Hurricanes will continue to batter the Gulf region. For coastal Louisiana and its residents, does any hope exist for a secure and sustainable future?

Coastal Restoration: Unfinished Business

Hopefully, the answer to the question will be "yes." Having recognized the problem, scientists and scholars, teachers and students, business and community leaders, and government officials are now working toward a solution. This effort includes education, outreach, and numerous projects of both large and small scale, designed to complement each other yet address the pressing needs of the areas in which they are located. Prior to hurricanes Katrina and Rita, these projects were encompassed in the Coast 2050 Plan and the Louisiana Coastal Area

Marshland erodes along the banks of the Barataria Waterway and nearby canals in the Deltaic Plain. The Barataria basin, which lies south of New Orleans, experiences one of the highest land loss rates in the coastal region. Courtesy of U.S. Army Corps of Engineers, New Orleans District.

An oil company supply boat speeds along a canal in the Chenier Plain. Bordering the canal is a spoil bank, a linear feature that provides high land for trees but also redirects the flow of water across the wetland.

Comprehensive Coastwide Ecosystem Restoration Study, or LCA. Since the hurricanes of 2005, these plans have evolved to include barrier defenses such as hurricane protection levees, floodgates, and elevated highways, along with the coastal restoration projects. Expanding the strategy to include both ecosystem restoration and hurricane protection has resulted in the Louisiana Coastal Protection and Restoration Authority's Comprehensive Master Plan for a Sustainable Coast. Although this multifaceted master plan is still in the early stages of implementation, a number of pre-

vious restoration efforts are evident in the coastal landscape.

Some of the small-scale projects that are visible to observers in the coastal zone are Christmas tree fences and terraces. These are usually located in areas of open water that once supported emergent vegetation but no longer do so because of subsidence or saltwater intrusion; in other words, they are located in former marshes that are now large ponds, shallow lakes, or bay edges. Their purpose is to provide a barrier that breaks the force of waves moving across the surface of the water; this helps reduce shoreline erosion and trap sediment, which can in turn reduce water depth and allow vegetation to take hold. A Christmas tree fence consists of a double row of posts that are sunk into the mud and designed to hold a community's discarded Christmas trees. Terraces are regularly spaced piles of earth often fashioned from discarded spoil; on them, plantings of salt-tolerant grasses send down roots to hold the terraces in place.

Plantings of vegetation are also essential in medium-scale coastal restoration efforts such as beach nourishment projects. Engineers pump sand from several miles offshore, replenishing the beach along threatened shorelines and barrier islands. This sand will not stay in place for long in such dynamic places, however; some will wash from the beach into the Gulf and its longshore current, which will transport it westward. Some will blow inland, forming low dunes that can be stabilized by hardy grasses like sea oats and bitter panicum. The dunes and remaining beach sand provide a measure of protection, along with an increased sediment supply to help sustain the fragile shore.

Beach nourishment projects often work together with segmented breakwaters, piles of huge limestone rocks that parallel the shoreline and reduce the force of incoming waves. Rather

Rows of terraces partition the shallow waters of Little White Lake in Vermilion Parish. The terraces will hopefully slow shoreline erosion and stabilize the banks of the navigation channel. Courtesy of U.S. Army Corps of Engineers, New Orleans District.

Four coastal restoration techniques—segmented rock breakwaters, beach nourishment, lines of sediment fences that trap blowing sand, and plantings of vegetation—are in use at Constance Beach in the western Chenier Plain.

than a continuous line of rocks, the breakwaters form a "dashed" line and allow water to flow around each end. In addition to reducing the force of the waves on the beach, the rocks trap sand and sediment; as a result, beaches sometimes appear to stretch outward toward the segmented breakwaters in a succession of sandy crescents.

Freshwater and sediment diversion efforts and marsh management with water control structures add a large-scale focus to the arsenal of coastal restoration techniques. Both of these methods are used throughout the coastal zone, but freshwater and sediment diversion projects are most useful in areas where waterways carry a heavy sediment load; accordingly, the largest projects are located in the Deltaic Plain. Structural marsh management attempts to reduce salt water's ingress into fresher areas by blocking waterways with gated or slotted barriers. Because saltwater intrusion is a major cause of coastal land loss in southwest Louisiana, this is the primary large-scale restoration technique in the Chenier Plain.

Freshwater and sediment diversions channel some of a river or bayou's water into areas of wetland in need of restoration. Along the Mississippi River, two major structures are currently operating: the Caernarvon project in St. Bernard Parish (east of New Orleans) and the Davis Pond project in Jefferson Parish (southwest of New Orleans). At these locations, a series of massive gates built into the levee allow water and sediment from the river to flow through con-crete channels and into deteriorating marshes. The gates can be adjusted to regulate volume of flow, recreating in a small area the historic annual flooding of the Mississippi River. The positive effects of this restoration technique are already evident in the wetlands near the Caernarvon project, which began operating in 1991. In these marshes, not only has water freshened and wildlife populations increased but pond edges are expanding and converting open water back to vegetated wetlands. The effects of the Davis Pond project, initiated in 2002, are expected to be equally promising.

The Davis Pond freshwater and sediment diversion project channels Mississippi River water beneath a highway and a railroad, then southward toward the swamps and marshes of the Barataria basin. Courtesy of U.S. Army Corps of Engineers, New Orleans District.

While people unfamiliar with these specific areas may not notice wetland growth or the actual freshwater and sediment diversion device, water control structures are more obvious in the wetland landscape. Large concrete structures with gates or slots to regulate the movement of water in a marshland bayou or canal are present in several federal and state wildlife refuges, while some refuges and privately owned wetlands feature smaller versions, including culverts with flap gates that can be raised or lowered. Birds and people often fish near these structures, for their presence can alter the movement of aquatic organisms, sometimes concentrating them at the structure as they seek a way to move into or out of the estuary.

Freshwater and sediment diversions, as well as large water control structures, are major engineering projects that take years to build and often create controversy. Costly and complex, they prioritize long-term interests such as coastal restoration and a sustainable ecosystem over short-term interests such as individual or family income or near-term wildlife and fisheries harvest. Accordingly,

The Grand Bayou water control structure in Cameron Prairie National Wildlife Refuge features a "boat bay" that allows fishermen and estuarine-dependent fish and shellfish access to the refuge's interior marshes. Refuge staff close the boat bay during periods of high water salinity and prior to hurricanes and tropical storms.

Visitors fish at a water control structure on Rockefeller State Wildlife Refuge, hoping for a bite as the water—and a variety of aquatic species—move between a small canal and the refuge marshes.

conflicts have arisen among some wetland residents, federal and state agencies, and environmental groups. One of the most notable of these conflicts developed as a result of the Caernarvon project, as area oyster harvesters successfully sued the state for damaging their oyster beds—and livelihoods—with the influx of freshwater into the oysters' brackish habitat. Such conflicts have added expense and challenge to the task of coastal restoration, but they have also resulted in valuable learning and a realization that in Louisiana's "work-

ing wetland," the interests of all those who use these lands and waters must be accommodated.

The Cost of Failing to Restore Louisiana's Coast: Lessons of Hurricanes Katrina and Rita

Among the many benefits that a wide band of coastal wetlands can provide is protection from hurricanes and associated storm surges. Marsh vegetation and swamp forests create friction that buffers surface wind speed and storm surge height. Coastal scientists estimate that for approximately every three miles of wetlands a storm surge crosses, the surge height is reduced by one foot. These specific benefits of healthy, intact coastal wetlands accrue not only to communities behind the wetland buffer but to the state and the nation as a whole, for the Louisiana coastal wetlands protect and harbor a major port, a bountiful seafood harvest, and a vital part of the U.S. energy supply infrastructure.

Previous Category 4 or 5 hurricanes such as Audrey in 1957, Betsy in 1965, and Camille in 1969 devastated communities near the shore, but more inland areas—including Lake Charles, Lafayette, Baton Rouge, and New Orleans, along with its levee system—were protected by the wetland buffer and spared the full fury of these storms. In the intervening decades, global climate has warmed (a harbinger of more intense storms and of sea level rise), population and energy consumption have increased, and Louisiana's wetlands have begun to disappear, especially in the Deltaic Plain. The "mental map" we have of a boot-shaped state is no longer accurate; the front of the boot's sole has come off, along with part of the foot, so that little more than the skeletal toes remain. (For more information on New Orleans's increased vulnerability as a result of coastal land loss,

see the articles "Drowning New Orleans" in *Scientific American,* October 2001, and "Gone with the Water" in *National Geographic,* October 2004.)

Into this setting of a tattered wetland, a heavily populated city where a large "wealth gap" exists between affluent and impoverished citizens, and a hot late summer, Hurricane Katrina roared ashore on Monday morning, August 29, 2005. The storm's center passed just east of New Orleans, devastating Biloxi and other Mississippi coastal communities with a storm surge of approximately twenty-five feet. On the Louisiana coast, the storm's eye crossed the mouth of the Mississippi River at Buras, surrounded by sustained winds of 145 miles per hour. Passing over an area that was once a wetland but is now mostly open water, the hurricane continued northward. Its strength unabated, Katrina's western eye wall soon engulfed New Orleans.

The counterclockwise circulation around the storm pushed a surge of water into Lake Pontchartrain—a surge that might have been of lesser intensity had the wetlands south and east of the city been intact and functioning as a storm surge buffer. By Tuesday morning, August 30, the pressure of high lake levels had caused three sections of the levee network to give way, slowly flooding the city of New Orleans—in some areas to a depth of twenty feet. The human

By August 30, the day after Hurricane Katrina struck, 80 percent of New Orleans was flooded. This view from Lake Pontchartrain's south shore area depicts the inundated city and, in the foreground, the yacht harbor at West End and the 17th Street Canal with its breached levee and floodwall. In the distance, the downtown New Orleans skyline is barely visible above a haze of heat and moisture. Courtesy of U.S. Army Corps of Engineers, New Orleans District.

Rooftops and a few tall trees rise above post-Katrina floodwaters in Lakeview, one of the New Orleans metropolitan area's most affluent and desirable subdivisions. Lakeview lies just east of the 17th Street Canal levee breach; the water that flowed through it stood for 2½ weeks, saturating homes and their contents, killing vegetation, and leaving a brown and desolate landscape. Like many other submerged areas, Lakeview has been slow to recover from the devastation. Courtesy of U.S. Army Corps of Engineers, New Orleans District.

Remnants of a shrimp boat sit in the front yard of a home on Oak Grove ridge after Hurricane Rita. Some of the chenier's live oak trees succumbed; others were completely or partially stripped of their leaves by the wind and storm surge.

suffering, death, devastation, and desperation that resulted from the inundation is likely well known to all readers; for me as a New Orleans native, it is too painful to reiterate.

What I do wish to communicate is that there is a broader context in which this disaster is embedded. It is the situation of coastal wetland loss in Louisiana and the imperative for coastal restoration, along with the federal assistance necessary to complete this vital task. The need and rationale for restoring Louisiana's wetlands should now be apparent to everyone who followed the saga of

Hurricane Katrina and its aftermath. To restore Louisiana's coastal wetlands will be an expensive task, but to rebuild the city of New Orleans without rebuilding the wetlands that are crucial for its survival will, in the long run, cost even more.

Less than a month after Hurricane Katrina, Hurricane Rita tore into the southwest Louisiana coast on September 23–24, 2005, devastating Chenier Plain communities from Johnson Bayou and Cameron to Grand Chenier and Pecan Island. In addition to rendering more than six thousand people homeless, the fifteen-foot

Hurricane Rita's storm surge came from the southeast and swept away much of the Chenier Plain's material culture, carrying residents' treasured possessions far to the northwest. This home floated approximately five miles across the flooded marshes of the Big Burn before coming to rest along Highway 27 west of Little Chenier.

People of all ages are recovering from the effects of the 2005 hurricanes. T-Mae Booth, whose home and business collapsed under the force of Hurricane Rita's winds and waters, is one of many chenier residents who have decided to rebuild. While their spirit and ties to the land are stronger than their fear of future storms, other survivors of hurricanes Rita and Katrina have chosen to relocate to more inland areas.

surge that crossed the region's eroding wetlands sent water farther inland than during any previous storm, raising lake and river levels and flooding parts of the inland cities of Lake Charles and Abbeville. Damages to the region's oil and gas infrastructure, added to those of Hurricane Katrina in southeast Louisiana, sent oil and natural gas prices soaring to record heights and will likely continue to affect the United States and its citizens.

The lessons of Hurricane Katrina and Hurricane Rita remind us that, while comprehensive coastal restoration will require an estimated fourteen billion dollars of federal funding, the failure to restore Louisiana's coast will certainly cost the nation much more. These costs will be measured not only in dollars but in human lives, energy availability, and quality of life.

CHAPTER 7

Visiting the Coast

Louisiana's coast is a place that surprises. On any given day, even those who have lifelong experience in these lands and on these waters will find something new to capture the imagination or spark a sense of wonder. Visitors to the region also sense its distinctiveness. They often express amazement not only at the beauty and diversity of these coastal wetlands but also at their sheer extent, for, even in decline, they remain one of the world's natural wonders.

This chapter details seasonal highlights, as well as locations where habitats such as swamps, marshes, cheniers, beaches, and barrier islands are open to the public for wildlife watching, photography, and other types of nature observation. Some of the larger areas, such as national wildlife refuges, also allow hunting, fishing, crabbing, and cast netting in season, by permit. Areas where these consumptive activities take place are often separate from those where other recreational activities occur, so visitors should always check with the refuge to determine which locations are designated for their activity of interest.

Each of the following regions features several destinations, and additional information on each is available via the Internet. Search under the specific place name for the site's current web address. Visitors who have an interest in birding may also wish to search for the "America's Wetland Birding Trail" online guide. This guide includes the places listed here, as well as additional locations suitable for observers who wish to spend more time and explore the regions in greater detail.

Seasons and Sensations

To fully experience the Louisiana coast, turn off the radio and other distracting devices, and allow your senses to absorb the region's sights, sounds, smells, and feelings. Each season has its special character. Summer's fishing and shrimping activities, lush green vegetation, breeding birds, dragonflies, and sultry evening choruses of frogs and toads give way by September to alligator trapping season, fall festivals, bright yellow wildflowers, and long-awaited cool fronts. As autumn progresses, each front brings new waves of ducks and geese, along with waterfowl hunters from across the nation.

By December the marshes, swamps, and coastal uplands are muted in color and subject to occasional freezing temperatures, but wintering waterfowl and other birds lure both hunters and wildlife watchers to the coast. The north winds and chilly conditions that follow the passage of cold fronts usually give way in two or three days to milder temperatures, until the next front arrives. During the coldest months, trappers work the wetlands in search of thickly furred nutria, muskrat, mink, and otter, though visitors will rarely notice this activity. More obvious is the marsh burning that landowners conduct to enhance vegetation growth, for it adds an occasional smoke plume and odor to the winter air.

Spring and its accompanying "green-up" commence in March, though cool fronts continue into April, and occasionally into early May. As the days lengthen and air temperatures begin to rise, spring bird migration begins. Ducks and geese make their way northward, away from the coast, while songbirds and shorebirds arrive, feed and rest for a time, then also journey north to breed. Many of the migratory songbirds are small and brightly colored; if they encounter unfavorable conditions such as north winds or rain as they travel across the Gulf of Mexico from their wintering areas in Mexico, Central America, and South America, the chenier and barrier island woods become a colorful spectacle of warblers, tanagers, orioles, and other migrants that land at the first available opportunity—the coastal edge. The promise of witnessing such a "fallout" draws birders from around the country and from other nations to the Louisiana coast each spring. The season's warmth also brings a renewed bloom of wildflowers, including native giant blue iris, along with a variety of butterflies and other insects that pollinate the flowers and tap their nectar. Scents of willow and honeysuckle perfume the air, later to be replaced by the sweet, light fragrance of Chinese tallow blossoms as spring merges into summer.

While each season presents a variety of delights, each also brings challenges, which visitors should prepare for. Summer's heat begins in May, when temperatures climb into the 80s. Although July and August temperatures rarely reach the mid-90s, the high humidity causes perspiration to remain on the skin rather than evaporating quickly and cooling

Summer's exuberant growth is evident in this brackish marsh on Rockefeller Refuge.

By late October, cattail flower spikes are becoming a cottony mass of seeds.

A male scarlet tanager (Piranga olivacea) *perches atop a barbed-wire fence during late April, the height of spring songbird migration.*

the body. Accordingly, summer visitors should carry and consume water in abundance and should consider wearing a hat and sunscreen. Winter weather can be surprisingly cold and penetrating, especially on rainy or humid days when a north wind is blowing. Under these conditions, even temperatures in the 40s can seem frigid, necessitating a hat, gloves, and coat. Biting insects, including mosquitoes and deerflies, are most prominent in warmer weather, but they can be bothersome any month of the year. Because of the threat of West Nile virus, health authorities suggest wearing long sleeves and long pants, a hat, and repellent to reduce insect bites.

With these opportunities and cautions in mind, here are some prospective destinations for visitors to the coastal wetlands, cheniers, and barrier islands. The list progresses from west to east and includes sites in the Chenier Plain, Deltaic Plain, and wetland areas north of New Orleans and east of Baton Rouge.

(left) Leaves of roseau frame a winter sunrise near Grand Chenier.

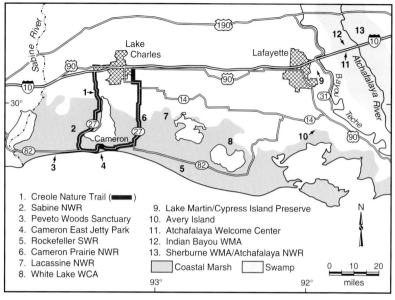

1. Creole Nature Trail (▬▬▬)
2. Sabine NWR
3. Peveto Woods Sanctuary
4. Cameron East Jetty Park
5. Rockefeller SWR
6. Cameron Prairie NWR
7. Lacassine NWR
8. White Lake WCA
9. Lake Martin/Cypress Island Preserve
10. Avery Island
11. Atchafalaya Welcome Center
12. Indian Bayou WMA
13. Sherburne WMA/Atchafalaya NWR

Coastal Marsh   Swamp

0   10   20
miles

N

Southwest and South Central Louisiana Coast

Southwest Louisiana Coast

This region of the state, the Chenier Plain, extends from the Texas border eastward to Vermilion Bay. The coast here features large expanses of marshland crossed by chenier ridges, ancient beaches that stand, isolated like islands, amid the grassy wetland and its wildlife. This area was devastated by Hurricane Rita's winds and storm surge, but many local residents and businesses are determined to retain their coastal land and culture. Visitors planning to explore the region can check for up-to-date information on the recovery via the Internet. Search under the following place names, as well as under "Cameron Parish" for the area's general and visitor information, including availability of lodging in and beyond the town of Cameron. For those visitors who wish to stay in a metropolis, Lake Charles lies just north of the Chenier Plain, while Lafayette is located to the northeast. Both provide a variety of accommodations, restaurants, and entertainment opportunities.

CREOLE NATURE TRAIL NATIONAL SCENIC BYWAY

Located halfway between Houston and New Orleans, the Creole Nature Trail is a 180-mile auto tour route that leaves Interstate 10 west of Lake

Charles (Exit 20) and rejoins I-10 east of the city (Exit 36). Following state highways 1256 and 27 west of Calcasieu Lake, highway 82 along the coast, and highways 27 and 397 east of Calcasieu Lake, the trail takes visitors through Sabine National Wildlife Refuge and Cameron Prairie National Wildlife Refuge, with options to extend the journey westward to Peveto Woods Sanctuary and eastward to Rockefeller State Wildlife Refuge. Visitors who complete the entire loop will pass through the communities of Sulphur, Hackberry, and Holly Beach on the western side of the trail,

as well as Holmwood, Sweet Lake, Creole, Oak Grove, and Cameron on the eastern side, across the Calcasieu Ship Channel. An additional community, Grand Chenier, lies along the eastern extension of the trail, across the Mermentau River. Convenience stores and groceries in these towns provide gasoline, provisions, and snacks and occasionally offer light meals. Because the towns are widely spaced, however, visitors should be sure to check fuel levels and carry some snacks and water as they set off to explore southwest Louisiana's coastal wetlands and cheniers.

An American alligator finds concealment amid floating pennywort (Hydrocotyle ranunculoides) *on Sabine National Wildlife Refuge.*

SABINE NATIONAL WILDLIFE REFUGE—WETLAND WALKWAY

Located approximately twenty-eight miles south of I-10's Exit 20 at Sulphur, the Wetland Walkway is a one-mile loop trail that offers easy access into the heart of a freshwater/intermediate marsh. This is an excellent place to explore the sights and sounds of the marsh at a leisurely pace, during any season of the year. The trail is hard surfaced or boardwalk for most of its length, and an observation tower affords a panoramic view of the wetland and nearby Calcasieu Lake. This is a good place to observe alligators in spring, summer, and fall.

PEVETO WOODS BIRD AND BUTTERFLY SANCTUARY

Peveto Woods is a small tract of chenier woodland protected from development by the Baton Rouge Audubon Society. The tract is located west of Holly Beach; turn south off Highway 82 at the Stingray gas plant. This turn takes visitors onto Gulf View Avenue and toward the Gulf of Mexico. Turn left (east) onto Tarpon Springs Avenue, and park at the end of the road, beyond which is the sanctuary. The chenier woods here are dominated by live oak and hackberry trees; also present are mulberry, honey locust, and additional trees and understory plants that provide food and shelter for birds, insects, and other wildlife. Peveto Woods is a good location for

birding, especially during spring migration. Access is free; donations are welcome.

CAMERON EAST JETTY PARK AND PIER

The town of Cameron, located along the Calcasieu River and ship channel, is the governmental seat of Cameron Parish and a major service center for the offshore oil and gas industry. While Louisiana Highway 82 parallels the coast and serves as Cameron's main street, many of the oilfield supply and service enterprises cluster along Davis Road (East Jetty Road), which turns south from Highway 82 just east of the Cameron water tower. At the end of this three-mile road are the massive rock jetties that guide vessels into and out of the Calcasieu Ship Channel, a busy water highway that connects the Gulf with the ports of Cameron and Lake Charles. Also located at the end of the road is East Jetty Park and Pier, an excellent location for fishing, boat watching, and nature observation. Although Hurricane Rita destroyed the park's structures in 2005, the parish plans to rebuild all facilities, including the fishing pier, picnic pavilion, RV parking area, and birding tower.

ROCKEFELLER STATE WILDLIFE REFUGE—PRICE LAKE ROAD

Diverging from Highway 82 one mile west of Rockefeller Refuge headquarters near the eastern end of

Searching for fall migrants, birders check the moss-draped oaks of a chenier woodland.

Grand Chenier, Price Lake Road is a three-mile-long, shell/limestone road that has long been a favorite crabbing, fishing, and cast-netting spot for residents and visitors. It is also a pleasant place to search for birds and alligators amid the refuge's brackish marshes and ponds. The Louisiana Department of Wildlife and Fisheries is steward of this refuge, and a Wild Louisiana Stamp (nonconsumptive use permit) or Louisiana hunting or fishing license is required for entry. A fishing license is required to fish, crab, or cast-net for shrimp. Stamps and licenses are available at most local convenience stores, as well as at sporting goods stores in cities adjacent to the coast.

CAMERON PRAIRIE NATIONAL WILDLIFE REFUGE—VISITOR CENTER AND PINTAIL WILDLIFE DRIVE

Cameron Prairie is the headquarters for the U.S. Fish and Wildlife Service's Southwest Louisiana National Wildlife Refuge Complex. The visitor center is located approximately seventeen miles south of I-10 (Exit 36), along Louisiana Highway 27 just south of Sweet Lake. The facility features exhibits, restrooms, and a boardwalk across a freshwater pond and surrounding marsh. Alligators and turtles are usually easy to spot here in the warmer months. Two miles south of the visitor center is the Pintail Wildlife Drive, a three-mile loop road through moist soil management units and shallow freshwater marsh. This is a good place to view ducks and geese in fall and winter.

LACASSINE NATIONAL WILDLIFE REFUGE—HEADQUARTERS AREA AND LACASSINE POOL

Located east of the Creole Nature Trail and southeast of Lake Charles, Lacassine Refuge is southwest Louisiana's third large federally owned property. Two areas on the refuge are accessible to visitors by road; both the headquarters area (and adjacent Streeter Road unit) and Lacassine Pool lie south of Louisiana Highway 14, between the communities of Hayes and Lake Arthur, which lie approximately ten and twelve miles south of I-10, respectively. Lacassine Pool is the westernmost area and is well worth a visit any time of the year. The large brown sign near a curve in Highway 14 east of Hayes directs visitors to the refuge via Illinois Plant Road, a four-mile journey through rice fields and pastures. At the end of this road is Lacassine Pool, a large freshwater marsh impoundment bordered by low earthen levees. Visitors can drive the road year-round, survey the marsh from an observation tower, fish from the bank, and launch small boats. Geese and ducks abound here in the cooler months, and migratory songbirds and shorebirds are numerous in spring and fall. In summer, the pool is an excellent place to see alligators, purple gallinules, white water lilies, and many other wetland species.

To the east of Lacassine Pool, the refuge headquarters area is much different in appearance, for it lies at the edge of the Mermentau River adjacent to a cypress-tupelo swamp. A short boardwalk and observation deck provide good wildlife viewing and photo opportunities. This is an excellent place to hear and observe northern parula and prothonotary warblers in spring and summer. Wood ducks are also present, and visitors occasionally glimpse black-bellied whistling ducks. The boardwalk is also a superb place to study the baldcypress and water tupelo trees that colonize low land at the river's edge. On the higher land, live oaks with Spanish moss line the entrance road to the headquarters building and parking area, which are well signposted and lie approximately four miles south of Highway 14, west of the community of Lake Arthur.

WHITE LAKE WETLAND CONSERVATION AREA
This recently acquired property of the Louisiana Department of Wildlife and Fisheries is an extensive freshwater marsh north of White Lake and south of the town of Gueydan, the next town east of Lake Arthur along Highway 14, where Highway 91 heads south toward the wetlands. This habitat is historically significant, for an isolated population of endangered whooping cranes nested in the White Lake marsh as late as the 1930s, and adult birds were present until 1950. Today it is one of the prime wintering areas for mallards, along with a variety of other ducks and large numbers of geese. In summer, a breeding colony of herons, egrets, ibises, cormorants, and roseate spoonbills adds sound and additional color to a stand of cypress trees near the White Lake Lodge. Pristine tallgrass prairie remains on a nearby ridge, while trees along the Gulf Intracoastal Waterway levee attract migratory songbirds in spring and fall. Long inaccessible to visitors while under the stewardship of a succession of oil companies (most recently British Petroleum–Amoco, which donated the property to the state), the White Lake Wetland Conservation Area is currently available for limited public use, and plans for additional access and environmental education programs are in the development stage. For the latest information, check the Louisiana Department of Wildlife and Fisheries website.

South Central Louisiana Coast

The Atchafalaya Basin, North America's largest river basin swamp, has long divided south Louisiana into

As the sky clears following a winter storm, a flock of ducks lifts from the marsh at the White Lake Wetland Conservation Area.

two distinct regions. To the west lies "Acadiana," the heartland of the Cajun culture, while to the east a more multicultural flavor is present, though heavily spiced with Cajun language, music, and surnames along the bayous of the Deltaic Plain. The Atchafalaya River is the Mississippi's first major distributary along its present course. Its waters and sediment have created a lowland landscape of cypress-tupelo swamps, lakes, intertwining rivers and bayous, bottomland hardwood forests, and a newly emerging delta. The following sites include locations in the western part of the Atchafalaya Basin and adjacent areas; all are located within an hour's drive of Lafayette, the "capital of Acadiana" and the region's largest city.

LAKE MARTIN—CYPRESS ISLAND PRESERVE

East of Lafayette along Interstate 10 is Breaux Bridge, a small town named for its bridge across Bayou Teche and renowned for its spring crawfish festival. A drive across the bridge takes visitors to Highway 31 and the turn south toward St. Martinville. Shortly after the road enters the rural area beyond the town, look for Lake Martin Road on the right. Turning here brings visitors to Lake Martin and the Louisiana Nature Conservancy's Cypress Island Preserve. Cypress Island is a good place to visit any time of year, but it can be spectacular from late winter through midsummer, when its wading bird rookery is active. During this time, the baldcypress and water tupelo trees that rise above the lake's still waters often host thousands of pairs of nesting birds, including several species of herons and egrets, plus roseate spoonbills, white ibises, anhingas, and neotropic cormorants. Until spring 2006, a large number of these birds were easily visible from the road along the lake's edge; their sudden abandonment of this area is still a mystery. Alligators, however, remain easy to see, for they are both large and abundant; their nests lie along the lake's southern shore, which is closed to foot traffic during the late spring and summer alligator breeding season.

Avery Island

South of Lafayette and Breaux Bridge is the city of New Iberia, and to its southwest, Louisiana Highway 329 brings visitors to Avery Island, a salt dome that towers 150 feet above the marshes of southern Iberia Parish. On this high land, the McIlhenny family established world famous Tabasco brand pepper sauce, and Edward Avery McIlhenny created the nesting platforms of "Bird City," which helped save snowy egrets from the relentless pressure of plume hunters in the early twentieth century. He also brought a variety of exotic plants from his world travels to create the island's "Jungle Gardens," which provide visitors with four miles of walking paths and driving trails to explore. Bird City lies within the Jungle Gardens; both are accessible for the same fee. The Tabasco manufacturing facility offers tours at an additional charge.

Atchafalaya Basin—Atchafalaya Welcome Center

Located at the Butte LaRose exit (Exit 121) on Interstate 10, the state welcome center on the western side of the Atchafalaya Basin is the appropriate starting point for any visit to the Atchafalaya region. The center features multimedia exhibits, printed information and helpful staff, restrooms, vending machines, and a pleasant area for walking and resting. Travelers who are interested in visiting the following two sites should check with center staff for information on road conditions, as roads through these areas may become muddy or impassible. Another option for experiencing the Atchafalaya Basin is to take a swamp tour by boat; the center staff can provide information on tours and approximate costs.

Herons, egrets, ibises, spoonbills, and cormorants roost and nest communally at a variety of locations in coastal Louisiana. These nesting birds are primarily great egrets and snowy egrets.

INDIAN BAYOU WILDLIFE MANAGEMENT AREA

From the Butte LaRose exit (Exit 121) on I-10, Louisiana Highway 105 leads north through the dense hardwood forests and cypress swamps of the Indian Bayou area. The U.S. Army Corps of Engineers owns and manages this area, which lies along either side of the road for seven miles. Birders will find the area interesting in all seasons, but the most impressive sightings for many come during the spring and summer breeding season, when swallow-tailed kites are nesting and rearing their young.

SHERBURNE WILDLIFE MANAGEMENT AREA AND ATCHAFALAYA NATIONAL WILDLIFE REFUGE

Like the Indian Bayou area, the Sherburne-Atchafalaya complex features bottomland hardwood forests and cypress swamps that harbor large numbers of breeding songbirds and several species of raptors, including swallow-tailed kites. Both the Sherburne area, owned by the Louisiana Department of Wildlife and Fisheries, and the Atchafalaya refuge, a property of the U.S. Fish and Wildlife Service, lie north of I-10 (Exit 127 at Whiskey Bay, east of Butte LaRose)

The base of an ancient baldcypress trunk dwarfs the birder in the canoe to its right. These vestiges provide clues to the size of trees in Louisiana's virgin cypress swamps before intensive logging felled them in the late nineteenth and early twentieth centuries.

along Louisiana Highway 975. The Louisiana Dept. of Wildlife and Fisheries requires visitors to obtain a Wild Louisiana Stamp (or Louisiana hunting or fishing license) prior to using the Sherburne area.

Southeast Louisiana Coast

The state's southeastern coastal region consists of the Mississippi River's broad Deltaic Plain, which includes varied habitats such as natural levees, bayous, cypress-tupelo swamps, marshes, beaches, mudflats, and barrier islands. Human activity in the region is as varied as are the habitats and includes wildlife and fisheries harvest, sugar cane and citrus agriculture, cattle ranching, industrial and port operations, tourism, and other service activities. The great river's birdfoot delta lies southeast of New Orleans, the region's largest and most notable metropolis. Having lost much of its protective barrier of wetlands, New Orleans is now, in effect, a coastal city. This section thus begins with two sites in the New Orleans metropolitan area before extending the focus "down the bayou" to the south, east, and west.

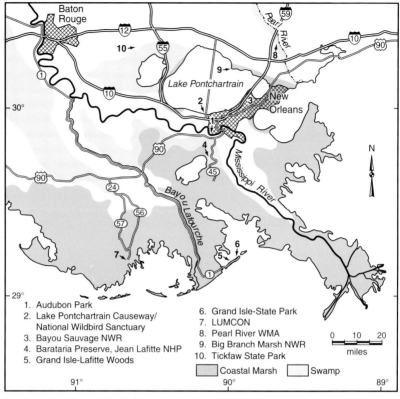

Southeast Louisiana Coast and Northshore

NEW ORLEANS—AUDUBON PARK
Located in the University Section of uptown New Orleans, Audubon Park stretches from the Mississippi River to St. Charles Avenue. Its stately live oaks and serpentine lagoon provide habitat for quiet recreation, as well as for wildlife. Wood ducks are present on the lagoon year-round, and in winter additional species join them. In the early 2000s, hundreds of wintering black-bellied whistling ducks added their distinctive, high-pitched whistling calls to the park's soundscape. In spring and summer, a variety of herons, egrets, and other wading birds use a small island on the park's east side to nest and raise their young. The trees in this vicinity also serve as a roosting site for the birds throughout the year.

*A juvenile purple martin (*Progne subis*) rests before beginning its first migration to South America, where it will spend the winter.*

LAKE PONTCHARTRAIN CAUSEWAY BRIDGE—NATIONAL WILDBIRD SANCTUARY

The twenty-four-mile Causeway Bridge that spans Lake Pontchartrain from north to south terminates on the south shore in the suburb of Metairie, just west of the city of New Orleans, at North Causeway Boulevard. Below the southernmost span of the bridge, approximately one hundred thousand purple martins roost each evening in mid- and late summer, as they stage for their southward migration. A group of local birders and purple martin aficionados developed "Proj-ect Swallow" to draw attention to the spectacle and enlist support for bird protection and habitat conservation at this important staging site. The project became the "National Wild-bird Sanctuary" and now features a viewing deck on the western side of the Causeway's south end, as well as fencing to protect the birds as they swoop across the bridge prior to en-tering the roost.

Barataria Preserve Unit, Jean Lafitte National Historical Park and Preserve

Twelve miles south of New Orleans's French Quarter lies a national treasure, an extensive cypress-tupelo swamp and marsh region rescued from urban expansion by the actions of a local schoolteacher and concerned citizen, Frank Ehret Jr. Today this twenty-thousand-acre wetland preserve is part of Jean Lafitte National Historical Park and features walking trails through bottomland hardwood forest, cypress-tupelo swamp, freshwater marsh edge, and canal bank habitat. Boardwalks traverse low, wet areas, so visitors' feet stay dry. The park also provides designated fishing areas, a visitor center, and an environmental education facility. The Bayou Coquille Trail and its extension, the Marsh Overlook Trail, traverse all of these habitats along their one-mile course. Chapter 2 includes a detailed description of these trails, which are excellent locations to view wetland fauna and flora, including the native giant blue iris in spring.

The Barataria Preserve is easy to reach from New Orleans by crossing the Mississippi River/Crescent City Connection bridge to the Westbank and exiting U.S. 90 at Barataria Boulevard, Louisiana Highway 45. Following Louisiana 45 south takes

Palmettos surround the aptly named Palmetto Trail in the Barataria Preserve.

visitors directly to the preserve; an alternate route along Louisiana 3134 (watch for signs for this newer road along Louisiana 45) will also take visitors to their destination, but it is less scenic than the old route along the bayou.

Bayou Sauvage National Wildlife Refuge

Located on the eastern side of Orleans Parish, entirely within the corporate limits of New Orleans, is the extensive Bayou Sauvage National Wildlife Refuge. The U.S. Fish and Wildlife Service manages the refuge, which encompasses freshwater and brackish marshes, ponds, canals, and bottomland hardwood forests along the banks of Bayou Sauvage, one of the Mississippi River's ancient courses. Drivers can view the refuge's upland habitats along U.S. 90 East/Chef Menteur Highway, just past the industrial areas and the Vietnamese community, approximately eight miles east of Interstate 10's Exit 240B. Wetland habitats stretch along U.S. 11, a north-south route that intersects U.S. 90 in the eastern part of the refuge.

For walkers, the refuge offers a half-mile boardwalk to the water's edge along the Ridge Trail, which passes through forest, palmettos, and a fringe of cypress swamp. A longer walk along the Maxent Levee often provides views of alligators, wading birds, mottled ducks in summer, and a variety of waterfowl in winter. The parking area for both trails is located in the westernmost part of the refuge, along U.S. 90/Chef Menteur Highway, on the north side of the road.

Grand Isle—Lafitte Woods Preserve and Grand Isle State Park

Located on the coast due south of New Orleans, Grand Isle is Louisiana's only road-accessible barrier island. The 110-mile drive to reach the island is well worth the effort, for the route traverses a variety of coastal habitats and also provides visible evidence of extensive wetland loss. The route begins across the Mississippi River from New Orleans, on the Westbank, where U.S. Highway 90 West passes through suburbs and small towns on the lower edge of the river's natural levee. As the highway turns away from the river, developed areas give way to backswamps where, among other things, the city's waste collection sites are located. The landscape changes as the road approaches the old German settlement of Des Allemands, located on a bayou of the same name, and eventually reaches the sugar cane processing town of Raceland. Here U.S. 90 meets Bayou Lafourche, a former Mississippi River course now plied by shrimp boats and a variety of other watercraft. Louisiana Highways 1 and 308 flank the bayou on its west and east sides,

These live oaks died decades ago as the natural levee along lower Bayou Lafourche subsided into the marsh. Today they stand above a sea of smooth cordgrass.

respectively. Highway 308 is the more rural of the two roads; it passes sugar cane fields and bayouside residences but dead-ends in Golden Meadow.

To reach Grand Isle, take Louisiana Highway 1, which passes through numerous small towns as it follows Bayou Lafourche, then continues south through miles of brackish and saltwater marshes to Cheniere Caminada, Caminada Bay, and Grand Isle. Along the route, note the skeletal remains of oak trees along the now-sunken banks of Bayou Lafourche just beyond Golden Meadow; the trees have died as a result of soil subsidence and saltwater intrusion caused by lack of sediment deposition and

fresh water flow. From atop the Leeville Bridge south of Golden Meadow, note the extensive area of open water before you. This large lake was a beautiful vegetated brackish marsh as recently as the 1960s.

Across the bridge spanning Caminada Pass lies Grand Isle, a seven-mile-long barrier island fronted by a sandy beach, backed by a fringe of saltwater marsh, and crowned by a live oak and hackberry forest at its center. Numerous camps and residences, several businesses and government buildings, a state park, and a woodland preserve dot the island and welcome visitors for day or overnight visits.

Many of the older tombs in the Grand Isle cemetery have French inscriptions. Behind the cemetery, a large Turk's cap shrub (Malvaviscus penduliflorus) is in flower. This is the larger of two varieties of Turk's cap (sometimes called sultan's turban); the smaller variety (Malvaviscus arboreus) has an upright red flower that resembles a Turkish fez.

Among areas to explore are the Lafitte Woods Preserve and Grand Isle State Park. Lafitte Woods—named after privateer Jean Lafitte, who frequented the island in the early 1800s—consists of several tracts managed by the Nature Conservancy. A small information kiosk and parking area are located on the north side of Highway 1 approximately four miles east of the island's bridge. The woodland tracts all lie north of the highway, in the central part of the island, including the area north of the Sureway Grocery. All are excellent birding sites, especially during spring and fall migration.

Swimmers and beachcombers, as well as birders, will enjoy visiting Grand Isle State Park, located at the eastern end of the island. The park charges a small entrance fee, but its amenities are numerous. Before the hurricanes of 2005, the park featured an observation tower, visitor center, nature trail, bathhouse, and fishing pier. Sandy beaches, a brackish lagoon, and Gulf waters continue to attract visitors while the park's infrastructure is under repair.

Louisiana Universities Marine Consortium (LUMCON)

The Louisiana Universities Marine Consortium lies approximately ninety miles south-southwest of New Orleans and thirty-one miles south of Houma, near the sport fishing village of Cocodrie (Louisiana Cajun French for "alligator"). Here visitors who have followed U.S. 90 West past Raceland to Houma and traveled south on Louisiana Highway 56 to its end will find not only alligators but also an educational and research facility with excellent exhibits, boardwalks, and an observation tower that overlooks the eroding brackish and saltwater marshes of the western Barataria-Terrebonne Estuary. Located nearly at land's end, LUMCON conducts a variety of marine research and educational programs and welcomes visitors at its De Felice Marine Center daily, excluding holidays. Admission is free; donations are welcome.

Southeast Louisiana: Northshore

While most visitors expect to find coastal habitats near the current shoreline, Louisiana's coast also includes the region north of lakes Maurepas, Pontchartrain, and Borgne, the three large lakes located north of New Orleans and east of Baton Rouge. These "Northshore" lowlands occur at the edge of pine-hardwood uplands and include bottomland hardwood forests and cypress-tupelo swamps, as well as freshwater and intermediate marshes. The first two sites in this section are closer to New Orleans than to Baton Rouge; the opposite is true for the final site. Each, however, lies within a half-hour drive of the nearest Interstate highway, and each offers visitors a variety of recreational opportunities.

Pearl River Wildlife Management Area and Honey Island Swamp

The Honey Island Swamp lies in the drainage basin of the Pearl River, which marks Louisiana's southeastern border with the state of Mississippi. Here meandering brown streams with sandy deposits on their banks rest below a thick canopy of bottomland hardwoods that harbor a variety of birds, especially during the breeding season. While swallow-tailed kites are sometimes visible as they soar overhead, most of the breeding birds—including prothonotary, Kentucky, and Swainson's warblers—announce their presence with their calls, for they are often difficult to spot among the thick vegetation. Swamps of baldcypress and water tupelo characterize areas of lower elevation and flank some of the access roads in the Wildlife Management Area (WMA).

The Pearl River WMA is located northeast of New Orleans near the town of Pearl River, just off Interstate 59 at the Old U.S. Highway 11 exit

Raised camps and recreational boats line the streets and canals of Cocodrie, a fishing village in the wetlands of Terrebonne Parish.

(Exit 5B). Travel northeast on Old U.S. 11 for approximately three miles to the WMA entrance station. The Louisiana Department of Wildlife and Fisheries requires a Wild Louisiana Stamp (or Louisiana hunting or fishing license) to enter the area; stamps and licenses are available from sporting goods stores in urban areas, as well as from some local convenience stores.

BIG BRANCH MARSH NATIONAL WILDLIFE REFUGE
Located north of New Orleans and south of Interstate 12 (Exit 74, Louisiana Highway 434), Big Branch Marsh National Wildlife Refuge is a short drive from the Northshore town of Lacombe. The refuge offers a visitor center with exhibits and educational programs, a short boardwalk nature trail through pine flatwoods, and a two-mile trail past freshwater marsh ponds and along the forest edge. Endangered red-cockaded woodpeckers nest in the pines here, and a variety of other birds, along with butterflies and dragonflies, reptiles, and amphibians frequent the trail area. Occasional sightings of large birds of prey include swallow-tailed kites in summer and bald eagles in winter. The refuge is also a good place to view wildflowers in spring, summer, and fall.

TICKFAW STATE PARK

The Northshore's pine-hardwood uplands give way to bottomland hardwoods and cypress-tupelo swamps as the land slopes gently toward the region's numerous creeks and rivers. All three habitats are present in Tickfaw State Park, which lies along the Tickfaw River near the small town of Springfield. The park is approximately thirty miles east of Baton Rouge via Interstate 12, then south on Louisiana 441 to Patterson Road, following the park signs. There is a small admission fee.

One of Louisiana's newest parks, Tickfaw State Park features nature trails and boardwalks through each of the preceding habitats, a nature center with exhibits and educational programs, cabins and campsites, canoe rentals, and fishing. In addition to the expected flora and fauna of the wetland areas, the park's drier uplands offer opportunities to view trees such as southern magnolia, American beech, winged elm, and flowering dogwood among the pines. The uplands, including the woodland edges near the entrance station, are good places to spot wild turkeys.

In a tranquil Northshore wetland, water hyacinths bloom beneath baldcypress, water tupelo, and southern wax myrtle (Myrica cerifera).

CHAPTER 8

Conclusion
Tenacity

On a cold winter afternoon several years ago, a flooded field along Illinois Plant Road near the Lacassine Refuge Pool was the setting for one of the most amazing displays of tenacity I have ever witnessed. Here, as the north wind rippled the water between the low rice field levees, a northern harrier repeatedly attacked an American coot, pouncing upon it and holding the bird underwater for minutes at a time. Occasionally one of the coot's black wings would lift above the surface and flail, but it seemed that the larger harrier, or marsh hawk, would win the struggle easily. Yet the coot bobbed back to the surface each time the harrier released its grip. After several repetitions of this scene, the hawk flew off, perhaps to seek easier, less tenacious prey. The coot rested for several minutes and then continued its feeding; it was impossible for me to determine the extent of its injuries.

Like the tenacious coot, the land and people of coastal Louisiana are engaged in a struggle that has life-or-death implications. Recent hurricanes have brought home the message that, without a barrier of healthy coastal wetlands, we will suffer damages similar to those that Hurricane Katrina and Hurricane Rita inflicted in 2005. Our way of life is already changing, as evacuations become more frequent and some longtime residents leave their homes for more inland areas. Lives will continue to change as eroding wetlands cease to protect ports and vital energy infrastructure and cease to nourish the state's multibillion-dollar seafood industry. These challenges of an eroding coast affect not only Louisianians, but people nationwide.

Yet despite the loss of approximately twenty-four square miles of wetlands each year, we are still here, clinging to our coast and providing the services associated with waterborne commerce, oil and gas production, seafood harvesting and processing, and recreation and tourism. Like the coot, we are tenacious; we continue on.

An American coot patters across a marshland pond, clearing the way for an approaching airboat.

There is precedent and inspiration for such tenacity in the example of the Acadians, who are ancestors of many south Louisiana residents and coastal dwellers. The Acadians were a French-speaking people torn from their northeastern North American homeland (today called Nova Scotia) in a brutal ethnic cleansing in 1755. Despite tremendous hardship, separation, and suffering, they tenaciously maintained their culture and family ties, and by 1785 they were refashioning a new homeland—and the beginnings of the Cajun culture—in the lowlands of south Louisiana.

But like the besieged coot, the extent of the damage to our coastal way of life, and to our long-term future here, is uncertain. Insurance coverage for homes and businesses is very expensive and harder to acquire; stricter building codes and elevation requirements add high costs to construction; and an economy and culture with deep roots in the wetlands will likely share the same fate as those ecosystems. As our marshes turn to open water and our cypress swamps blanch and fall, will we be like that last clump of marsh grass in a widening bay, hanging on in the face of in-

At the Alligator Harvest Festival, Elizabeth Richard displays pride in her Louisiana coastal heritage and in the region's wildlife.

A brackish marsh slowly erodes on Rock-efeller Refuge.

surmountable odds, as the saltwater rises?

The Louisiana coast and its people are vital, valuable, and vulnerable. They are both contributors and creators, enriching the country's culture and economy with fertile lands and waters, hard work, and a unique blend of language, food, music, customs, and an enviable *joie de vivre*. Here lies a "working wetland" second to none on the continent of North America, perhaps second to none on Earth. A unique place on the southern rim of the United States, the Louisiana coast is worth cherishing, worth protecting, and worth saving, but it will take the commitment and support of the entire nation to achieve this goal.

The beauty and promise of the Louisiana coast are manifest in the wetland landscape of Marsh Island. Courtesy of U.S. Army Corps of Engineers, New Orleans District.

Books and Other Resources to Enhance Your Wetland Experience

The following sections list books, articles, videos, and Internet sites that offer additional information on topics and issues presented in this guide. The books include recent works, as well as a few "classics" from earlier decades. Most of the recent items are still in print, and many of the books and videos are also available in libraries. Producers and sponsoring organizations appear after each video title; their websites often provide a synopsis of the program, as well as instructions for ordering VHS or DVD copies. While web addresses sometimes change, the organizations associated with the sites usually appear in Internet search engines, affording readers access to the information in its new location.

Regions, People, and Life on the Louisiana Coast

America's Wetland: Louisiana's Vanishing Coast, Bevil Knapp and Mike Dunne (Baton Rouge: Louisiana State University Press, 2005)

Vanishing Paradise: Duck Hunting in the Louisiana Marsh, John Kemp and Julia Sims (Gretna, La.: Pelican, 2004)

Marsh Mission: Capturing the Vanishing Wetlands, C. C. Lockwood and Rhea Gary (Baton Rouge: Louisiana State University Press, 2005)

National Wetlands Research Center, http://www.nwrc.usgs.gov

CHENIER PLAIN

A Wetland Biography: Seasons on Louisiana's Chenier Plain, Gay M. Gomez (Austin: University of Texas Press, 1998)

DELTAIC PLAIN

Bayou Farewell: The Rich Life and Tragic Death of Louisiana's Cajun Coast, Mike Tidwell (New York: Vintage, 2003)

Rising Tide: The Great Mississippi Flood of 1927 and How It Changed America, John M. Barry (New York: Simon and Schuster, 1997)

"Haunted Waters, Fragile Lands: Oh, What Tales to Tell!" [video], Glen

Pitre, producer (Barataria-Terrebonne National Estuary Program, 1996, 2001) http://www.btnep .org

Barataria-Terrebonne National Estuary Program, http://www.btnep .org

ATCHAFALAYA BASIN

Cajun Families of the Atchafalaya: Their Ways and Words, Greg Guirard (St. Martinville, La.: Author, 1989, rev. ed. 1999)

Designing the Bayous: The Control of Water in the Atchafalaya Basin, 1800–1995, Martin Reuss (College Station: Texas A&M University Press, 2004)

Atchafalaya: America's Largest River Basin Swamp, C. C. Lockwood (Baton Rouge: Claitor's, 1984)

NEW ORLEANS AND HURRICANE KATRINA

An Unnatural Metropolis: Wresting New Orleans from Nature, Craig E. Colten (Baton Rouge: Louisiana State University Press, 2004)

1 Dead in Attic: After Katrina, Chris Rose (New York: Simon & Schuster, 2007)

1 Dead in Attic: Post-Katrina Stories by Times-Picayune *Columnist Chris Rose,* Chris Rose (New Orleans: Chris Rose Books, 2005) http:// www.chrisrosebooks.com

The Storm: What Went Wrong and Why during Hurricane Katrina—

The Inside Story from One Louisiana Scientist, Ivor van Heerden and Mike Bryan (New York: Viking, 2006)

The Great Deluge: Hurricane Katrina, New Orleans, and the Mississippi Gulf Coast, Douglas Brinkley (New York: William Morrow, 2006)

Path of Destruction: The Devastation of New Orleans and the Coming Age of Superstorms, John McQuaid and Mark Schleifstein (New York: Little, Brown, 2006)

Katrina: The Ruin and Recovery of New Orleans, New Orleans *Times-Picayune* (New Orleans: Times-Picayune, LLC; Champaign, Illinois: Spotlight Press [distributor], 2006)

"The Storm That Drowned a City," [video], *Nova* episode, November 22, 2005 (PBS [Public Broadcasting Service]) http://www.pbs.org

PRE-KATRINA WARNINGS

"Drowning New Orleans," Mark Fischetti, *Scientific American* (October 2001), pp. 76–85

"Gone with the Water," Joel K. Bourne Jr., *National Geographic* (October 2004), pp. 88–105

CAJUN CULTURE AND HISTORY

The Founding of New Acadia: The Beginnings of Acadian Life in Louisiana, 1765–1803, Carl A. Brasseaux (Baton Rouge: Louisiana State University Press, 1987)

Cajun Country, Barry Jean Ancelet, Jay Edwards, and Glen Pitre, Folklife in the South series (Jackson: University Press of Mississippi, 1991)

"Against the Tide: The Story of the Cajun People of Louisiana," [video], Zachary Richard, producer (Louisiana Public Broadcasting, c. 2000) http://www.lpb.org, http://www.zacharyrichard. com

Vegetation

Common Vascular Plants of the Louisiana Marsh, R. H. Chabreck and R. E. Condrey (Baton Rouge: Louisiana State University Center for Wetland Resources, 1979) Sea Grant publication no. LSU-T-79-003

Aquatic and Wetland Plants of the Western Gulf Coast, Charles D. Stutzenbaker (Austin: Texas Parks and Wildlife Press, 1999)

Natural Resources Conservation Service, PLANTS Database, http://plants.usda.gov

Louisiana State University Agricultural Center, http://www.lsuagcenter.com

Barataria-Terrebonne National Estuary Program, http://www.btnep.org

WILDFLOWERS

Wildflowers of Louisiana and Adjoining States, Clair A. Brown (Baton Rouge: Louisiana State University Press, 1972)

The Louisiana Iris: The Taming of a Native American Wildflower, Marie Caillet, J. Farron Campbell, Kevin C. Voughn, and Dennis Vercher, eds. (Portland, Ore.: Timber Press, 2000)

TREES

Louisiana Trees and Shrubs, Clair A. Brown (Baton Rouge: Claitor's, 1972)

National Audubon Society Field Guide to North American Trees, Eastern Region, Elbert L. Little Jr. (New York: Knopf, 1980)

Forest Trees of the United States and Canada, and How to Identify Them, Elbert L. Little Jr. (New York: Dover, 1979)

Nature, Culture, and Big Old Trees: Live Oaks and Ceibas in the Landscapes of Louisiana and Guatemala, Kit Anderson (Austin: University of Texas Press, 2004)

Baldcypress: The Tree Unique, the Wood Eternal, Clair A. Brown (Baton Rouge: Claitor's, 1986)

Wildlife

A note about wildlife field guides: Several suggestions are included in the following lists, but sometimes the best way to choose a field guide is to visit the nature section of your favorite bookstore and browse their selection, examining different guides to determine which will best serve your level of interest and experience. Generally, those guides that describe a species, illustrate it (preferably with paintings that show male, female, and juvenile, when appropriate), and include a map of its range *all on the same page* are easier to use than guides that place this information in different sections of the book.

BIRDS

Field Guide to the Birds of North America, National Geographic Society (Washington, D.C.: National Geographic Society, 2002)

Birds of North America, Kenn Kaufman, Kaufman Focus Guides series (New York: Houghton Mifflin, 2000)

The Sibley Guide to Birds, David Allen Sibley, National Audubon Society (New York: Knopf, 2000)

Birds of the Gulf Coast, Brian K. Miller and William R. Fontenot (Baton Rouge: Louisiana State University Press, 2001)

Louisiana Birds, George H. Lowery (Baton Rouge: Louisiana State University Press, 1974)

The Return of the Brown Pelican, Dan Guravich and Joseph E. Brown (Baton Rouge: Louisiana State University Press, 1983)

"Wings over the Wetlands" [video], Michelle Benoit and Glen Pitre, producers (Barataria-Terrebonne National Estuary Program, 2001) http://www.btnep.org

Louisiana Ornithological Society, http://www.losbird.org

LARGER MAMMALS

The Mammals of Louisiana and Its Adjacent Waters, George H. Lowery (Baton Rouge: Louisiana State University Press, 1974)

Handbook of Mammals of the South-Central States, Jerry R. Choate, J. Knox Jones Jr., and Clyde Jones (Baton Rouge: Louisiana State University Press, 1994)

Louisiana Fur and Alligator Advisory Council, http://www.alligatorfur.com

Louisiana State University Agricultural Center, http://www.lsuagcenter.com (Environment and Natural Resources section)

Louisiana Department of Wildlife and Fisheries, http://www.wlf.louisiana.gov

BUTTERFLIES, DRAGONFLIES, AND OTHER INSECTS

A Field Guide to Eastern Butterflies, Paul A. Opler, Peterson Field Guide series (New York: Houghton Mifflin, 1992)

Butterflies through Binoculars: The East, Jeffrey Glassberg (New York: Oxford University Press, 1999)

Stokes Beginner's Guide to Dragonflies and Damselflies, Blair Nikula and Jackie Sones, with Donald and Lillian Stokes (New York: Little, Brown, 2002)

Dragonflies through Binoculars, Sidney W. Dunkle (New York: Oxford University Press, 2000)

Louisiana State University Agricultural Center, http://www.lsuagcenter.com (Environment and Natural Resources section)

Reptiles and Amphibians

The Amphibians and Reptiles of Louisiana, Harold A. Dundee and Douglas A. Rossman (Baton Rouge: Louisiana State University Press, 1989, 1996)

The Alligator Book, C. C. Lockwood (Baton Rouge: Louisiana State University Press, 2002)

Louisiana Fur and Alligator Advisory Council, http://www.alligatorfur.com

Louisiana Amphibian Monitoring Program, http://www.wlf.louisiana.gov, or access Louisiana information through the North American Amphibian Monitoring Program, http://www.pwrc.usgs.gov/naamp

Fish and Shellfish

Freshwater Fishes of Louisiana, Neil H. Douglas (Baton Rouge: Claitor's, 1974)

Fishes of the Gulf of Mexico: Texas, Louisiana, and Adjacent Waters, H. Dickson Hoese and Richard H. Moore (College Station: Texas A&M University Press, 1998)

Beachcomber's Guide to Gulf Coast Marine Life, Susan B. Rothschild (Lanham: Taylor, 2004)

Wetland Loss and Restoration

No Time to Lose: Facing the Future of Louisiana and the Crisis of Coastal Land Loss (Baton Rouge: Coalition to Restore Coastal Louisiana, 2000) http://www.crcl.org

Coast 2050: Toward a Sustainable Coastal Louisiana, Louisiana Coastal Wetlands Conservation and Restoration Task Force and the Wetlands Conservation and Restoration Authority (Baton Rouge: Louisiana Department of Natural Resources, 1998) http://www.lacoast.gov

Integrated Ecosystem Restoration and Hurricane Protection: Louisiana's Comprehensive Master Plan for a Sustainable Coast, Louisiana Coastal Protection and Restoration Authority (Baton Rouge: Louisiana Coastal Protection and Restoration

Authority, 2007) http://www.loui
sianacoastalplanning.org

*America's Wetland: Louisiana's Vanish-
ing Coast,* Bevil Knapp and Mike
Dunne (Baton Rouge: Louisiana
State University Press, 2005)

*Bayou Farewell: The Rich Life and
Tragic Death of Louisiana's Cajun
Coast,* Mike Tidwell (New York:
Vintage, 2003)

*Holding Back the Sea: The Struggle for
America's Natural Legacy on the
Gulf Coast,* Christopher Hallowell
(New York: HarperCollins, 2001)

*Saving Louisiana? The Battle for
Coastal Wetlands,* Bill Streever
(Jackson: University Press of Mis-
sissippi, 2001)

*The Ravaging Tide: Strange Weather,
Future Katrinas, and the Coming
Death of America's Coastal Cities,*
Mike Tidwell (New York: Free
Press, 2006)

"Drowning New Orleans," Mark
Fischetti, *Scientific American,* (October 2001), pp. 76–85

"Gone with the Water," Joel K.
Bourne Jr., *National Geographic*
(October 2004), pp. 88–105

"America's Vanishing Treasure"
[video], Craig Gautreaux, producer (Barataria-Terrebonne National
Estuary Program, 2000) http://
www.btnep.org

"Haunted Waters, Fragile Lands: Oh,
What Tales to Tell!" [video], Glen
Pitre, producer (Barataria-Terre-

bonne National Estuary Program,
1996, 2001), http://www.btnep
.org

National Wetlands Research Center,
http://www.nwrc.usgs.gov

America's Wetland: Campaign to Save
Coastal Louisiana, http://www
.americaswetland.com

Coalition to Restore Coastal Louisiana, http://www.crcl.org

Louisiana Coastal Restoration Web
site "LaCoast," http://www
.lacoast.gov

Louisiana Coastal Protection and Restoration Authority, http://www
.louisianacoastalplanning.org

Louisiana Department of Natural
Resources, http://www.dnr.louisi
ana.gov (Coastal Restoration and
Management section)

Barataria-Terrebonne National Estuary Program, http://www.btnep
.org

Visiting the Coast

Louisiana Office of Tourism, http://
www.crt.louisiana.gov

Louisiana State Parks, http://www
.crt.louisiana.gov/parks

Louisiana Department of Wildlife and
Fisheries (for info on state refuges
and wildlife management areas),
http://www.wlf.louisiana.gov

U.S. Fish and Wildlife Service (for
info on national wildlife refuges),

http://www.fws.gov/refuges

Atchafalaya Heritage Area, http://www.atchafalayatrace.org

America's Wetland Birding Trail Guide, http://www.louisiana travel.com/explorela/outdoors/birding (Access also available through http://www.losbird.org or http://www.americaswetland .com)

Bibliography

Ancelet, Barry Jean, Jay Edwards, and Glen Pitre. *Cajun Country.* Folklife in the South series. Jackson: University Press of Mississippi, 1991.

Barras, J. A., S. Beville, D. Britsch, S. Hartley, S. Hawes, J. Johnston, P. Kemp et al. *Historical and Projected Coastal Louisiana Land Changes 1978–2050.* U.S. Department of the Interior, U.S. Geological Survey. USGS Open File Report 03-334. Revised January 2004.

Barras, J. A., P. E. Bourgeois, and L. R. Handley. *Land Loss in Coastal Louisiana 1956–1990.* National Biological Survey, National Wetlands Research Center. USGS Open File Report 94-01, 1994.

Bernard, Shane K. "M'sieu Ned's Rat? Reconsidering the Origin of Nutria in Louisiana: The E. A. McIlhenny Collection, Avery Island, Louisiana." *Louisiana History* 43 (Summer 2002): 281–93.

Bourne, Joel K., Jr. "Gone with the Water." *National Geographic* (October 2004): 88–105.

Brasseaux, Carl A. *The Founding of New Acadia: The Beginnings of Acadian Life in Louisiana, 1765–1803.* Baton Rouge: Louisiana State University Press, 1987.

Brown, Clair A. *Baldcypress: The Tree Unique, the Wood Eternal.* Baton Rouge: Claitor's, 1986.

———. *Louisiana Trees and Shrubs.* Baton Rouge: Claitor's, 1972.

———. *Wildflowers of Louisiana and Adjoining States.* Baton Rouge: Louisiana State University Press, 1972.

Cahoon, Donald R., and Charles G. Groat, eds. *A Study of Marsh Management Practice in Coastal Louisiana.* New Orleans: U.S. Department of the Interior, Minerals Management Service, 1990. OCS Study MMS 90-0075.

Chabreck, Robert H. *Coastal Marshes: Ecology and Wildlife Management.* Wildlife Habitats series, ed. Milton W. Weller. Minneapolis: University of Minnesota Press, 1988.

———. *Vegetation, Water, and Soil Characteristics of the Louisiana Coastal Region.* Baton Rouge: Louisiana State University Agricultural Experiment Station, 1972. Bulletin no. 664.

————, and R. E. Condrey. *Common Vascular Plants of the Louisiana Marsh.* Baton Rouge: Louisiana State University Center for Wetland Resources, 1979. Sea Grant publication no. LSU-T-79-003.

Choate, Jerry R., J. Knox Jones Jr., and Clyde Jones. *Handbook of Mammals of the South-Central States.* Baton Rouge: Louisiana State University Press, 1994.

Coalition to Restore Coastal Louisiana. *No Time to Lose: Facing the Future of Louisiana and the Crisis of Coastal Land Loss.* Baton Rouge: Coalition to Restore Coastal Louisiana, 2000.

Coleman, James M. *Recent Coastal Sedimentation: Central Louisiana Coast.* Baton Rouge: Coastal Studies Institute, Louisiana State University, 1966. Technical report no. 29.

Din, Gilbert C. *The Canary Islanders of Louisiana.* Baton Rouge: Louisiana State University Press, 1988.

Douglas, Neil H. *Freshwater Fishes of Louisiana.* Baton Rouge: Claitor's, 1974.

Dundee, Harold A., and Douglas A. Rossman. *The Amphibians and Reptiles of Louisiana.* Baton Rouge: Louisiana State University Press, 1989, 1996.

Elsey, Ruth M. "Uncovering the American Alligator." *Louisiana Conservationist* (September/October 2002), reprint.

Fischetti, Mark. "Drowning New Orleans." *Scientific American* (October 2001): 76–85.

Frazier, David E. "Recent Deltaic Deposits of the Mississippi River: Their Development and Chronology." *Transactions, Gulf Coast Association of Geological Societies* 17 (1967): 287–315.

Gomez, Gay M. "Roots in the Wetlands." *Historical Geography* 31 (2003): 31–40.

————. *A Wetland Biography: Seasons on Louisiana's Chenier Plain.* Austin: University of Texas Press, 1998.

Gosselink, James G., Carroll L. Cordes, and John W. Parsons. *An Ecological Characterization Study of the Chenier Plain Coastal Ecosystem of Louisiana and Texas.* 3 vols. Slidell, La.: U.S. Fish and Wildlife Service, Office of Biological Services, 1979. FWS/OBS-78/9 through 78/11.

Gould, H. R., and E. McFarlan Jr. "Geologic History of the Chenier Plain, Southwestern Louisiana." *Transactions, Gulf Coast Association of Geological Societies* 9 (1959): 261–70.

Guirard, Greg. *Cajun Families of the Atchafalaya: Their Ways and Words.* St. Martinville, La.: Author, 1989.

Guravich, Dan, and Joseph E. Brown. *The Return of the Brown Pelican.* Baton Rouge: Louisiana State University Press, 1983.

Hallowell, Christopher. *Holding Back the Sea: The Struggle for America's Natural Legacy on the Gulf Coast.* New York: HarperCollins, 2001.

Hoese, H. Dickson, and Richard H. Moore. *Fishes of the Gulf of Mexico: Texas, Louisiana, and Adjacent Waters.* College Station: Texas A&M University Press, 1998.

Joanen, Ted. "Nesting Ecology of Alligators in Louisiana." *Proceedings, Annual Conference, Southeastern Association of Game and Fish Commissioners* 23 (1969): 141–51.

———, and Larry McNease. "Notes on the Reproductive Biology and Captive Propagation of the American Alligator." *Proceedings, Annual Conference, Southeastern Association of Game and Fish Commissioners* 29 (1975): 407–15.

———, Guthrie Perry, David Richard, and Dave Taylor. "Louisiana's Alligator Management Program." *Proceedings, Annual Conference, Southeastern Association of Fish and Wildlife Agencies* 38 (1984): 201–11.

Kniffen, Fred B., and Sam Bowers Hilliard. *Louisiana: Its Land and People.* Baton Rouge: Louisiana State University Press, 1988.

Little, Elbert L., Jr. *Forest Trees of the United States and Canada, and How to Identify Them.* New York: Dover, 1979.

Louisiana Amphibian Monitoring Program, Louisiana Department of Wildlife and Fisheries. Training CD with Louisiana frog and toad calls, c. 2000, courtesy of Avery Williams, Louisiana State University–Eunice.

Louisiana Coastal Protection and Restoration Authority. *Integrated Ecosystem Restoration and Hurricane Protection: Louisiana's Comprehensive Master Plan for a Sustainable Coast.* Baton Rouge: Louisiana Coastal Protection and Restoration Authority, 2007.

Louisiana Coastal Wetlands Conservation and Restoration Task Force. "Freshwater Diversions: Revitalizing Louisiana's Coastal Wetlands." Special issue. *WaterMarks: Louisiana Coastal Wetlands Planning, Protection, and Restoration News.* August 2003.

———. "Vegetative Plantings." Special issue. *WaterMarks: Louisiana Coastal Wetlands Planning, Protection, and Restoration News.* April 2005.

———, and the Wetlands Conservation and Restoration Authority. *Coast 2050: Toward a Sustainable Coastal Louisiana, an Executive Summary.* Baton Rouge: Louisiana Department of Natural Resources, 1998.

Louisiana Department of Culture, Recreation, and Tourism. *Explorer's Map of the Atchafalaya Heritage Area.* Baton Rouge: Louisiana Department of Culture, Recreation, and Tourism, Atchafalaya Trace Commission, c. 2004.

Louisiana Department of Natural Resources. *America's Energy Corridor: Louisiana Serving the Nation's Energy Needs.* Baton Rouge: Louisiana Department of Natural Resources, 2006.

———. "Louisiana Coastal Facts." http://www.dnr.louisiana.gov. 2007.

———. State Coastal Zone Boundary. SONRIS-GIS database. http://www.dnr.louisiana.gov. 2007.

Louisiana Department of Transportation and Development. "Official Map of Louisiana." Baton Rouge: Louisiana Department of Transportation and Development, 2000.

Louisiana Department of Wildlife and Fisheries. *Poisonous Snakes and Harmless Snakes of Louisiana.* Baton Rouge: Louisiana Department of Wildlife and Fisheries, 1980. Wildlife Education Bulletin nos. 9 and 10.

———, Fur and Refuge Division. *Fur Animals, Alligator, and the Fur Industry in Louisiana.* Baton Rouge: Louisiana Department of Wildlife and Fisheries, 1987.

Louisiana Office of Tourism. *America's Wetland Birding Trail on Louisiana's Great Gulf Coast.* Trail guides for loops 1–12. Baton Rouge: Louisiana Office of Tourism, 2005.

Louisiana State University Agricultural Center. *Wetlands Functions and Values in Louisiana.* Baton Rouge: Louisiana State University Agricultural Center/Louisiana Cooperative Extension Service, 1994. Publication 2519.

Lowery, George H. *Louisiana Birds.* Baton Rouge: Louisiana State University Press, 1974.

———. *The Mammals of Louisiana and Its Adjacent Waters.* Baton Rouge: Louisiana State University Press, 1974.

Miller, Brian K., and William R. Fontenot. *Birds of the Gulf Coast.* Baton Rouge: Louisiana State University Press, 2001.

Morton, R. A., N. A. Buster, and M. D. Krohn. "Subsurface Controls on Historical Subsidence Rates and Associated Wetland Loss in South-central Louisiana." *Transactions, Gulf Coast Association of Geological Societies* 52 (2002): 767–78.

Nikula, Blair, and Jackie Sones, with Donald and Lillian Stokes. *Stokes Beginner's Guide to Dragonflies and Damselflies.* New York: Little, Brown, 2002.

O'Neil, Ted. *The Muskrat in the Louisiana Coastal Marshes.* New Orleans: Louisiana Department of Wild Life and Fisheries, 1949.

Opler, Paul A. *A Field Guide to Eastern Butterflies.* Peterson Field Guide series. New York: Houghton Mifflin, 1992.

Penfound, William T., and Edward S. Hathaway. "Plant Communities in the Marshlands of Southeastern Louisiana." *Ecological Monographs* 8 (January 1938): 51–54.

Rand McNally. *Atlas of World Geography.* New York: Rand McNally, 2003.

Raynie, R. C., and S. K. Beasley. *Working to Save Our Coastal Wetlands.* Public information brochure. Baton Rouge: Louisiana Department of Natural Resources, Coastal Restoration Division, 2000.

Reuss, Martin. *Designing the Bayous: The Control of Water in the Atchafalaya Basin, 1800–1995.* College Station: Texas A&M University Press, 2004.

Russell, R. J., and H. V. Howe. "Cheniers of Southwestern Louisiana." *Geographical Review* 25 (July 1935): 449–61.

Saucier, Roger T. *Geomorphology and Quaternary Geologic History of the Lower Mississippi Valley.* Vicksburg, Ms.: U.S. Army Engineers, Waterways Experiment Station, 1994.

Sibley, David Allen. *The Sibley Guide to Birds.* National Audubon Society. New York: Knopf, 2000.

Stutzenbaker, Charles D. *Aquatic and Wetland Plants of the Western Gulf Coast.* Austin: Texas Parks and Wildlife Press, 1999.

Tidwell, Mike. *Bayou Farewell: The Rich Life and Tragic Death of Louisiana's Cajun Coast.* New York: Vintage, 2003.

U.S. Army Corps of Engineers, NOD [New Orleans District]. "Long-term Relative Subsidence Rates Derived from Radiocarbon Dating of Buried Peat Deposits." U.S. Army Corps of Engineers, New Orleans District, 1995. Map (digital image) in Reprographics Section, New Orleans District office.

U.S. Department of Agriculture, Natural Resources Conservation Service. "The PLANTS Database." Baton Rouge: National Plant Data Center, 2007. http://plants.usda .gov.

U.S. Geological Survey, National Wetlands Research Center. "USGS Reports Latest Land Change Estimates for Louisiana Coast." Press release. Lafayette, La.: National Wetlands Research Center, October 3, 2006. http://www.nwrc .usgs.gov.

Yodis, Elaine G., and Craig E. Colten. *Geography of Louisiana.* New York: McGraw Hill, 2007.

Index